Contents

About the Authors vii

Acknowledgments ix

Introduction 1
      Components of the *PLAI* Curriculum
      Guiding Principles
      Target Population
      Background Required for Effective Use of the Curriculum
      Role of Service Providers
      Implementing the Curriculum
      Getting Started

Module 1: Understanding Your Child's Cues 11

Module 2: Identifying Your Child's Preferences 25

Module 3: Establishing Predictable Routines 33

Module 4: Establishing Turn Taking 51

Module 5: Encouraging Communicative Initiations 61

Final Note 72

References 73

vi   Contents

Appendix A: Using Videotaped Observations 75
Appendix B: Data Collection and Recording Sheets 81
Appendix C: Background, Development, and Field-Test of the Curriculum 85
Appendix D: Handouts in English 89
    Overview of Module Goals and Objectives
    Overview of Module Goals and Recording Sheets
    Important Questions (for the Service Provider)
    PLAI Caregiver Interview
    Case Study: Michael's Story
    Module 1 Handouts
    Module 2 Handouts
    Module 3 Handouts
    Module 4 Handouts
    Module 5 Handouts

Appendix E: Handouts in Spanish 145
    PLAI Entrevista para el Cuidador del Niño/a
    Análisis de un caso: La Historia de Miguel
    Module 1 Handouts
    Module 2 Handouts
    Module 3 Handouts
    Module 4 Handouts
    Module 5 Handouts

Promoting Learning Through Active Interaction

Promoting Learning Through Active Interaction

A Guide to Early Communication with Young Children Who Have Multiple Disabilities

by

M. Diane Klein, Ph.D., CCC-SLP
California State University–Los Angeles

Deborah Chen, Ph.D.
California State University–Northridge

and

Michele Haney, Ph.D.
California State University–Northridge

Baltimore • London • Toronto • Sydney

Paul H. Brookes Publishing Co.
Post Office Box 10624
Baltimore, Maryland 21285-0624

www.brookespublishing.com

Copyright © 2000 by Paul H. Brookes Publishing Co., Inc.
All rights reserved.

Typeset by Pro-Image Corporation, York, Pennsylvania.
Manufactured in the United States of America by Bang Printing, Brainerd, Minnesota.

The project on which this book is based was funded in part by the U.S. Department of Education Research to Practice Grant #H0225S40001 to California State University–Northridge. The content, however, does not necessarily reflect the position of the U.S. Department of Education, and no official endorsement should be inferred.

Purchasers of *Promoting Learning Through Active Interaction: A Guide to Early Communication with Young Children Who Have Multiple Disabilities* are granted permission to photocopy the recording sheets and other forms that appear in this book for clinical/educational purposes. None of these pages may be reproduced to generate revenue for any program or individual. Photocopies must be made from an original book.

The case studies described in this book are composites based on the authors' experiences; these case studies do not represent the lives or experiences of specific individuals, and no implications should be inferred.

Two accompanying videos, *Promoting Learning Through Active Interaction: An Instructional Video* and *Promoviendo el aprendizaje a través de la interacción activa: Un video instruccional,* can be purchased separately. To order, contact Paul H. Brookes Publishing Co., P.O. Box 10624, Baltimore, Maryland 21285-0624 (1-800-638-3775; www.brookespublishing.com).

Text was translated into Spanish by Christina Pruess, M.A., and Gloria Rodriguez-Gil, M.Ed.
Cover photographs courtesy of Lavada Minor, M.A., Claire Taylor Friedman, Ph.D., and Gloria Rodriguez-Gil, M.Ed.

Permission is gratefully acknowledged to use graphics/images appearing in the margins courtesy of ClickArt ® Incredible Image Pak™, copyright ©1996 The Learning Company, Inc. and its subsidiaries. All rights reserved. Used by permission. ClickArt, Image Pak, and Brøderbund are trademarks and/or registered trademarks of Learning Company Properties, Inc.

Library of Congress Cataloging-in-Publication Data
Klein, M. Diane.
    Promoting learning through active interaction: a guide to early communication with young children who have multiple disabilities / by M. Diane Klein, Deborah Chen, Michele Haney.
       p.   cm.
     Includes bibliographical references.
     ISBN 1-55766-464-1
     1. Handicapped children—Care—Study and teaching. 2. Handicapped children—Education. 3. Communication in education—Study and teaching. 4. Handicapped—Means of communication—Study and teaching. I. Chen, Deborah. II. Haney, C. Michele, 1944— III. Title.

HV888 .K57   2000
362.4´048´083—dc21
                                                                                     00-027234

British Library Cataloguing in Publication data are available from the British Library.

About the Authors

M. Diane Klein, Ph.D., CCC-SLP, Professor and Chair, Division of Special Education, California State University–Los Angeles, 5151 State University Drive, Los Angeles, California 90032-4226

Dr. Klein studied speech pathology and audiology at Western Michigan University and received her doctorate in developmental psychology from Michigan State University. She has had a wide range of experiences with children with disabilities, including children with severe and multiple disabilities. She also has years of experience as a university instructor and clinical supervisor in the fields of communication disorders and special education. She is currently Professor and Chair of the Early Childhood Special Education Department at California State University–Los Angeles, where she coordinated the credential, master's, and certificate programs in infancy and early childhood special education. These programs emphasize the training of early intervention personnel to work in urban multicultural environments. In addition to her work at the university, Dr. Klein frequently conducts in-service training in the areas of communicative skills for children with disabilities, curriculum development in early childhood special education, and inclusion support strategies.

Dr. Klein has directed numerous federal grant projects, including Project Support, a project to develop training models and materials related to inclusion support skills and methods in early childhood special education. She has conducted research in the area of mother–infant communication and has developed early intervention programs that serve families at high risk, including the Mother–Infant Communication Project. She is author or co-author of several texts, including *Adapting Early Childhood Curricula for Children in Inclusive Settings* (Merrill, 2000). Dr. Klein has two books in press with Delmar: *Including Children with Special Needs in Early Childhood Programs: Activities and Strategies* (2001) and *Working with Young Children From Culturally Diverse Backgrounds* (co-authored with Deborah Chen, 2001). She serves on numerous boards and committees related to early intervention services in the state of California and is Executive Director of Centro De Niños y Padres Intervention Program.

Deborah Chen, Ph.D., Professor, Department of Special Education, California State University–Northridge, 18111 Nordhoff Street, Northridge, California 91330-8265

Dr. Chen received her master's degree and teaching credentials in special education from San Francisco State College and received her doctorate in special education with a minor in developmental psychology from the joint doctoral program at the University of California–Berkeley and San Francisco State University. She has been a teacher of school-age children with severe and multiple disabilities, an early interventionist with infants who have visual impairments or are deaf or deaf-blind, and an administrator of programs for these children in California. Dr. Chen has directed several federally funded projects related to professional development in early intervention/early childhood special education and program development for infants with multiple disabilities and sensory impairments. She has worked with families of diverse cultural and linguistic backgrounds. Her research and publications have focused on caregiver interactions with infants who have disabilities, early communication in infants with multiple disabilities and sensory impairments, interventions for these infants and preschoolers, and effective practices for working with families of diverse cultures. Dr. Chen has provided leadership in developing in-service training models and materials in these areas of professional development in California and other states. At California State University–Northridge, Dr. Chen teaches in the master's and credential programs in Early Childhood Special Education. She has been invited to conduct courses in early intervention practices for working with children who have multiple disabilities and sensory impairments throughout the United States, Australia, Canada, the Netherlands, Taiwan, and Thailand. Dr. Chen's recent publications include *Conversations for Three* (Paul H. Brookes Publishing Co., 2000), a videotape for service providers and interpreters working together; *Essential Elements in Early Intervention: Visual Impairments and Multiple Disabilities* (AFB Press, 1999); and *Working with Young Children From Culturally Diverse Backgrounds* (co-authored with M. Diane Klein, Delmar, 2001).

Michele Haney, Ph.D., Associate Professor, Department of Special Education, California State University–Northridge, 18111 Nordhoff Street, Northridge, California 91330-8265

Dr. Haney completed her undergraduate degree at Goddard College in Plainfield, Vermont; earned her master's degree in educational administration at Castleton State College in Castleton, Vermont; and received her doctorate in special education at California State University–Los Angeles and the University of California–Los Angeles. Her initial work as an early childhood educator included developing programs to serve children with disabilities and children at risk for disabilities within existing preschool and child care programs using the consulting teacher model. Her interest in young children with emerging developmental delays brought her to the Marianne Frostig Center for Children with Learning Disabilities, where she developed a program for preschool-age children at risk for later learning problems. Dr. Haney has co-directed or coordinated a number of national demonstration, preservice, and in-service training programs designed to increase the skills of individuals working with young children who have disabilities. Her research, focused on behaviors facilitating parent–child interactions, has most recently addressed increasing communication between parents and their infants who are deaf-blind. Dr. Haney's recent publications include *Preschool Inclusion* (co-authored with Claire C. Cavallaro, Paul H. Brookes Publishing Co., 1999).

Acknowledgments

Promoting Learning Through Active Interaction—Project PLAI reflects a 4-year collaboration involving California State University–Northridge, SKI*HI Institute at Utah State University, early intervention programs, service providers, and families of infants whose multiple disabilities include visual impairment and hearing loss. The development and field testing of these materials would not have been possible without the families, their children, service providers, and administrators who participated in the project in southern California and Utah. Special thanks to the families and service providers of the Infant–Family Program of the Foundation for the Junior Blind, the Los Angeles Unified School District Infant Program for Deaf and Hard of Hearing Infants, the Los Angeles Unified School District Parents and Infants with Visual Impairments Together (PIVIT), the Early Start Program of the Santa Barbara County Office of Education, and the Early Intervention Deaf-Blind Services for the Utah School for the Deaf and the Blind. Our gratitude to Virginia and Summer Barmeyer, Amy Christopherson and Angelika Clemens, Myrna and Norman Medina, and Juan Carlos and Rosa Salas for permission to include their photos. Special thanks to Michael and Amy Daly for helping us remember Elizabeth.

We appreciate the work of several part-time staff who contributed to the success of Project PLAI. We acknowledge the efforts of Beverly Simkin, project coordinator, and Suzanne Hendley, administrative assistant, who participated in the early years of the project. Particular recognition goes to Lavada Minor, project coordinator, and Christina Pruess, bilingual coordinator, whose teamwork and skills enabled the implementation and evaluation of the curriculum with English- and Spanish-speaking families. Special appreciation goes to Aileen Domingo, administrative assistant, whose good nature, effective organization, and competent clerical skills contributed to a timely completion of the project materials. We are grateful to Linda Alsop and Rosemary Vandermayden for coordinating replication efforts in Utah and to Gloria Rodriguez-Gil for working on Spanish translations.

We also recognize the support of Charles W. Freeman of the Office of Special Education and Rehabilitative Services, U.S. Department of Education, the project's federal program officer. Our appreciation goes to California State University–Northridge and the SKI*HI Institute at Utah State University for hosting Project PLAI.

Our appreciation goes to the team at Paul H. Brookes Publishing who made the *PLAI* materials a reality. In particular, we recognize Heather Shrestha, Lisa Rapisarda, Kimberly Murphy, Amy Kopperude, January Layman-Wood, Roslyn Udris, Paula Sloman, Erin Geoghegan, and Lisa Yurwit for their good ideas, expertise, and patience.

Introduction

The *Promoting Learning Through Active Interaction (PLAI)* curriculum is designed primarily for infants, preschoolers, and young children with severe or multiple disabilities who are not yet initiating symbolic communication and who have a limited repertoire of communicative behavior. It can also be used with older children who have not yet developed intentional communication. The *PLAI* curriculum promotes active interactions among caregivers, children, and their service providers while addressing these goals:

1. Developing a clear understanding of the child's existing repertoire of cues and behaviors
2. Understanding the child's likes and dislikes and current means of communication
3. Increasing the number, frequency, and clarity of the child's communicative behaviors
4. Strengthening the interactive relationship between the caregiver and the child

One of the most challenging areas of development for children with severe and multiple disabilities (particularly for those who have hearing loss or visual impairment) is the development of communication skills. This area of development is critical for several reasons. First, communication skills are important to the overall development and life satisfaction of the child. Equally important is the critical role of communication in the development of attachment and the ongoing relationship between caregiver and child. In children who develop typically, communication and language skills unfold easily in natural environments, within the context of naturally occurring interactions between the child and caregivers. In most cases for children who have mild to moderate disabilities, the most optimal "intervention" and support for the development of communication skills is simply the enhancement of naturally occurring interactions.

For children who have multiple disabilities and sensory impairments, however, the challenge is somewhat greater. Although the potential for the development of communication skills exists, in most cases it will not occur without very careful planning and implementation of specific intervention strategies. Because the communicative behaviors of a child with severe or multiple disabilities may be infrequent and are often subtle and atypical, busy caregivers may have a difficult time identifying and enhancing them.

Thus, many of the strategies described in this curriculum are necessarily highly structured and require systematic observations that are analyzed into small pieces of behavior. However, despite the curriculum's use of very specific strategies, these strategies must be adapted so that they can be incorporated into the daily activities and home routines of each child and his or her family.

The goal of the curriculum is for caregivers to become very sensitive to their child's communicative repertoire and potential and to develop strategies that can eventually be incorporated easily into daily interactions with their child. The term *caregivers* refers not only to a child's parents but also to family members, child care workers, and other people who are involved in the child's daily care.

COMPONENTS OF THE *PLAI* CURRICULUM

The *PLAI* curriculum is composed of the *Caregiver Interview*, a means of identifying the child's current communicative behaviors and interactional skills, and five modules. Each of the modules includes a rationale, a goal, directions to the service provider, and objectives and procedures. Each objective is broken down into steps to guide you through the curriculum. Real-life examples and completed recording sheets illustrate *PLAI* at work. A pencil graphic in the left margin will let you know when you'll need to use a recording sheet. Special points to remember are called out in Notes that are interspersed throughout the text. (See figure on the opposing page for a summary of the goals and objectives for each module.) The strategies for each module are demonstrated in a video (Chen, Klein, & Haney, 2000) that has an accompanying discussion booklet. The video is available in English and in Spanish.

GUIDING PRINCIPLES

The *PLAI* curriculum reflects an integration of three critical guiding beliefs, principles, key concepts, and theoretical perspectives in developmental psychology:

1. Responsive interaction with primary caregivers is the most significant factor in a child's early development.
2. A caregiver's ability to observe, interpret, and respond accurately to the child's cues and behavior will enhance the child's development.
3. Communication skills provide an essential foundation for all learning.

The curriculum is also based on several key intervention principles. First, children with severe and multiple disabilities learn best through:

- Predictable and meaningful routines
- Repeated opportunities to participate actively in everyday activities
- Opportunities to receive meaningful, consistent cues and ample time to respond
- Opportunities to initiate interaction
- Carefully planned, systematic, and fine-tuned intervention during everyday activities

Second, caregivers and service providers can facilitate the child's learning by using the following strategies:

- Carefully and systematically observing the child

Module 1: Understanding Your Child's Cues

Goal	Objectives
Caregivers will have a detailed picture of the ways in which the child expresses attention and interest, internal states such as pleasure and discomfort, and needs and desires.	1. Caregivers will describe the child's typical day. 2. Caregivers will learn to identify the child's different states. 3. Through careful observation of antecedent events and consequences, caregivers will develop a clear understanding of the child's typical reactions to routines and activities. 4. Caregivers will identify and describe ways in which the child obtains attention from the caregiver and for what purposes. 5. Caregivers will describe how the child reacts to and expresses external states and feelings.

Module 2: Identifying Your Child's Preferences

Goal	Objectives
Caregivers will develop a thorough understanding of what the child enjoys and what he or she dislikes.	1. Caregivers will generate a detailed list of people, objects, and activities that they believe the child enjoys and those the child dislikes. 2. Caregivers will describe the child's reaction to the presentation and removal of specific people, objects, and activities.

Module 3: Establishing Predictable Routines

Goal	Objectives
Caregivers will create a daily routine that includes several predictable events that the child can anticipate through recognition of certain cues such as sounds, sights, or other sensations.	1. Caregivers will identify at least five daily activities that can be scheduled in the same sequence each day. 2. Caregivers will identify predictable sequences within specific activities, or *subroutines*. 3. Caregivers will identify specific auditory, visual, tactile, olfactory, and kinesthetic cues that can be used to help the child anticipate familiar activities and daily events.

Module 4: Establishing Turn Taking

Goal	Objectives
The child will participate in familiar turn-taking routines in which he or she can interact easily with caregivers.	1. Using information gained in previous modules, caregivers will learn how to encourage the child to request more of a desired food or event. 2. Caregivers will identify and extend any current turn-taking routines and create new turn-taking games through initiation. 3. Caregivers will generalize turn-taking games across people and settings.

Module 5: Encouraging Communicative Initiations

Goal	Objectives
The child will increase his or her rate of initiations for the purposes of obtaining a desired object or pleasurable event and expressing rejection.	1. Caregivers will learn how to increase the child's initiations by encouraging the child to express rejection of a disliked object or activity. 2. Caregivers will learn to increase the child's initiations by delaying an anticipated event. 3. Caregivers will learn how to encourage the child to initiate intentionally and to obtain the caregiver's attention.

- Providing predictable routines
- Establishing accurate interpretations and providing contingent responses to the child's cues
- Building on the child's preferences and interests to motivate communication
- Providing enough time for the child to respond
- Making input meaningful through consistent, appropriately paced experience

The user of this curriculum should be familiar with several intervention concepts including the following:

Appropriate pacing: Timing interactions and input to engage and to maintain the child's attention and interest; avoiding rapid speech rate or rapid shifting from one event to another; providing ample wait time for the child to respond.

Contingent responsivity: Responding immediately to the child's behavior

Contingent stimulation: Giving the child stimulation as a consequence of his or her own behavior (i.e., the child looks and reaches, and the music box lights up and plays)

Meaningful input: Providing sensory information that is accessible to the child and that promotes his or her understanding of the ongoing activity or situation

Scaffolding: Providing supports to facilitate a fit between the child's abilities and the particular activity (i.e., prompts, adaptive devices, environmental and activity modifications)

Turn taking: Responding to the child's behavior—a turn—followed by some reciprocal behavior on the part of the child (e.g., the child kicks his or her legs, caregiver responds by vocalizing and blowing on the child's tummy, then child kicks his or her legs again, and so forth). There is an equal distribution of turns.

Two theoretical perspectives on early development and learning provide a basis for this curriculum, the transactional model and the concept of the child's zone of proximal development. The transactional model (Sameroff & Chandler, 1975) views developmental outcome as a consequence of reciprocal interactions between a child and the caregiving environment. The child, his or her family, and their environment influence each other, and a child's optimal development is the result of ongoing and successful adjustments within these relationships. The child's zone of proximal development—the next developmental step for that child—is the difference between what a child can do independently and what that child can accomplish with caregivers' assistance (Vygotsky, 1978).

Caregivers can aid the development of a child with severe and multiple disabilities through careful use of selected interventions that support the child's participation in, interaction with, and understanding of the social and physical environment. This will support the child's development of the ability to engage in the various transactions that are so critical to learning. In addition to the child's development, caregivers can learn that the child with severe and multiple disabilities needs additional time and specific—sometimes unique—scaffolds in order to learn.

The *PLAI* curriculum focuses on promoting the child's interaction within the context of the family's daily routine, thus addressing the importance of supporting caregiver–child interactions in culturally responsive ways (McCollum & McBride, 1997). Further, strategies emphasize the skills that both the caregiver and the child bring to the interaction, with intervention building on existing strengths (rather than focusing on deficits) and supporting the natural efforts of caregivers (Chen, 1996).

Introduction

TARGET POPULATION

The *Promoting Learning Through Active Interaction (PLAI)* curriculum is intended for use with infants, preschoolers, and older children who are developmentally very young and who are functioning at a "preintentional" level of communicative development. This includes children with severe or multiple disabilities; children whose behavioral responses and communicative cues are subtle, ambiguous, or inconsistent; and children with disabilities who do not engage in reciprocal interactions. The curriculum focuses on:

- Observing and interpreting the child's behaviors and states
- Establishing predictable routines
- Using systematic cues
- Establishing turn taking
- Encouraging the child's communicative initiation

Given its focus, this curriculum is not the best choice for the child who demonstrates clear, intentional communicative behaviors such as pointing, directed reaching, eye gaze, and differentiated noncry vocalizations and who intentionally initiates interaction and readily engages in turn-taking games.

Adaptations for Older Children

These curriculum strategies can also be used with older children who function at an early communication level. However, selected activities should be adapted for age appropriateness and the instructional context should include both home, school, and community environments. For example, Recording Sheet 1-A: Typical Daily Activities should be completed for home, school, and community environments. The implementation of the *PLAI* curriculum requires regular contact and discussion between the service provider and caregivers. This may require more family–school collaboration than exists currently between a teacher and the family of an older student; regular contacts will be needed. The *PLAI* curriculum may also serve as a mechanism for more coordinated interdisciplinary teaming as well, involving not only special education teachers from a variety of areas but also occupational and physical therapists, speech-language therapists, behavior specialists, and psychologists. Older children with severe disabilities may have a wider repertoire of current communicative behaviors than infants and preschoolers. Their behavioral signals may be more consistent and obvious. However, older children may also have developed challenging behaviors as a means of communication that interfere with learning new ways of communicating. For example, they may have learned to elicit attention through self-abusive behaviors. Finally, without early opportunities to experience contingent responses to a variety of communicative behaviors and to develop a sense of control, older students may have more deeply entrenched patterns of learned helplessness, may appear more passive, and may be less responsive to interactions.

BACKGROUND REQUIRED FOR EFFECTIVE USE OF THE CURRICULUM

The *PLAI* curriculum is intended to be used by trained early childhood special educators and other service providers working with caregivers, families, and their children who have severe disabilities. It assumes that service providers have a basic understanding and competence in the following areas:

- Typical early development of young children
- Characteristics and developmental challenges associated with specific disabilities
- The importance of caregiver–child interaction in supporting the child's development of attachment and healthy emotional development, as well as the development of language and cognition
- The use of basic teaching strategies such as scaffolding, task analysis, and applied behavior analysis
- The use of specific interaction strategies that facilitate the development of communication skills
- The use of play, daily caregiving activities, and predictable routines as contexts for teaching and learning
- The ability to establish effective family–professional partnerships
- The ability to collaborate with other service providers working with the child and family
- The ability to support caregivers in promoting their child's development
- An understanding of the influence of culture on family values and child-rearing practices

ROLE OF SERVICE PROVIDERS

The primary role of the service provider in implementing this curriculum is to coach the child's significant caregivers as they develop positive interaction strategies and routines. The service provider seeks to enable the caregiver to develop effective strategies that will become so well established that they are used automatically throughout all activities of the child's daily routine.

In the role of coach, the focus of the service provider is not to work directly with the child, except when modeling for the caregiver. Rather, it is to work in partnership with the family and caregivers in developing a deeper understanding of how the child experiences the world and of the meaning of the child's behaviors.

To explain each module effectively, the service provider must become very familiar with the curriculum. It is essential that the service provider read each module carefully, practice introducing the concept, review relevant forms, and be thoroughly familiar with the concepts. He or she must also use the examples included in each module to introduce the concepts and activities. Modeling includes actual demonstration of the strategy described in the module, as well as, in some cases, videotaping the child or the caregiver and child together depending on which module is being demonstrated. (Guidelines for videotaping can be found in Appendix A.) These videotapes can be examined for examples of certain child behavior, to carefully analyze sequences of events, to demonstrate positive caregiver–child interactions, and so forth.

Monitoring the caregiver's and the child's progress through the curriculum can be a challenging feature for some service providers. Nevertheless, for many children with severe and multiple disabilities, it is extremely difficult, if not impossible, to identify and to understand subtle or infrequent behaviors or to determine the effects of a particular strategy without monitoring via careful data recording. Examples of completed recording sheets are included in relevant modules. The service provider should tailor the data collection process to meet the needs and preferences of each family. (See Appendix B for a more detailed consideration of this topic.)

In order to carry out the role of coach successfully, it will also be necessary for the service provider to learn how to explain, model, and monitor the techniques and activities described in each training module. This way he or she can truly assist caregivers and support the child's development.

IMPLEMENTING THE CURRICULUM

The approach and strategies presented in this curriculum should be infused into the child's existing intervention program. First, the model of working in partnership with families and other caregivers and promoting caregiver–child interaction, whether in a home-based or center-based context, should be established as the primary framework, and then the other *PLAI* components should be incorporated into it. Second, it is essential that the family and the child's team of service providers discuss the *PLAI* curriculum and identify how to infuse strategies throughout the child's day. Young children with severe and multiple disabilities may receive services from a single service provider or from a variety of service providers who represent a range of disciplines (e.g., visual impairment, hearing loss, deafblindness, occupational therapy, physical therapy, and early childhood special education). Selection of specific strategies should involve the child's service providers from a variety of disciplines, for example, in creating anticipatory cues as discussed in Module 3. Further, the information gathered (e.g., the child's preferences, dislikes, states of arousal, and reactions to daily activities) in each of the five modules will be useful to all service providers in their own interactions and interventions with the child.

Although the curriculum is highly structured, it must be implemented within naturally occurring events. If the activities and strategies are time consuming and unnatural, few families will be able to use them. The modules and goals in this curriculum are presented in a very specific sequence. It is generally recommended that activities be presented in the order described, although the pace of moving through the modules is set by each family's circumstances.

It is important to realize that communication events occur as integrated, multidimensional wholes, not as isolated components. Unfortunately, it is impossible to teach caregivers to understand and observe all the dimensions of communication simultaneously. Thus, initially it is necessary to teach each component separately. It will quickly become obvious that these components overlap substantially. Families must complete Modules 1 and 2 before moving to later modules. Modules 1 and 2 are the most difficult because they require observation rather than action. Nevertheless, it is crucial that caregivers initially spend time carefully observing their child.

Feedback from many caregivers during field-test activities has indicated that even though they spend every day with the child and feel they know the child well, their time is primarily spent engaging in the often complex demands of basic caregiving. (For more information about field-test findings, please see Appendix C.) Caregivers have commented that the observation activities in the first two modules have taught them patience and provided the opportunity to observe their child in a new light.

However, once the first two modules have been completed, there may be some cases in which the service provider feels that modules should be presented in a different order. This is most likely to occur, for example, when a caregiver discovers the value of pausing and waiting for a request for "more" from the child (Module 4) before completion of

Establishing Predictable Routines (Module 3), or when the child begins initiating for attention (Module 5) while working on Module 4. However, it is important that families have the opportunity to develop the skills and strategies from all modules. Without being rigid and inflexible, the service provider will need to determine whether all key components of the curriculum have been addressed.

GETTING STARTED

Before using the *PLAI* curriculum, service providers should first gather pertinent background information on the individual child by using multiple data sources, such as reviewing available reports, interviewing caregivers, and consulting with other service providers and relevant professionals. The *Important Questions* sheet on page 10 should be used to guide the service provider in gathering relevant information. (These questions can also be found in Appendixes D and E of this book.) Service providers should answer these questions based on a synthesis of information from reports, other service providers, and the child's family. In this way, service providers will have an overall picture of the child's learning needs and will have begun the process of collaborating with the child's family and other involved service providers.

Next, service providers should complete the *Caregiver Interview* (see Appendixes D and E) in discussion with caregivers. The purpose of this interview is to gather information about how the child communicates by providing a structure for a conversation with the caregiver. The interview form may be used 1) as a baseline measure before beginning the curriculum, 2) for describing how the child reacts to external states and expresses feelings, and 3) after the caregiver has completed the curriculum. A comparison of these data on the *Caregiver Interview* should identify any change in the child's communication and in the caregiver's observations and so evaluate the effectiveness of the curriculum.

Introducing the Curriculum to Families

Because the curriculum has some complex and unfamiliar aspects, how the curriculum is initially introduced to caregivers is important. A one-page overview of each module is provided at the beginning of each module section and in Appendixes D and E for service providers to discuss with caregivers. When the curriculum was field tested, parents and some service providers indicated they had difficulty understanding the importance of some strategies in the beginning modules or how each module was connected. The case study of Michael (see Appendixes D and E) was developed in order to describe the curriculum process for service providers and for caregivers who like written materials. Also, service providers can use the simple script when introducing the curriculum to families. Service providers may also use the accompanying *PLAI* videotape (Chen, Klein, & Haney, 2000), available in English (close captioned) or Spanish, to demonstrate key strategies of the curriculum to families.

Initial Explanation of the Curriculum to Caregivers

After gathering information about the child's learning style and needs and completing the *Caregiver Interview*, service providers should introduce the *PLAI* curriculum to caregivers through a simple explanation of its purpose and procedures. Here is a script that you can use with modifications for each child (i.e., inserting the child's name instead of saying "your child" and using the appropriate pronoun instead of saying "he or she"):

PLAI Explanation

Children who are born with severe or multiple disabilities or who develop them later present unique challenges. This is especially true when those disabilities include the loss of vision or hearing. Their behaviors are often inconsistent and difficult to understand. They do not learn in the same way as children without these challenges, and they need very specific kinds of help in order to reach their potential. Fortunately, in recent years we have learned a great deal about the best ways to help infants and other children who have such disabilities. This curriculum incorporates much of this research to teach parents and caregivers how to support and understand their child's development. It is designed to help you in four ways. First, it can help you to better understand the meaning of your child's behaviors and how he or she experiences the world. Second, the curriculum can teach you how to use systematic cues and predictable routines to help your child learn to understand what is happening around him or her. Third, it can help you learn to use specific strategies to teach and to improve your child's communication skills. Finally, it can help you learn how to describe your child's unique skills and behaviors to members of your family and community.

The curriculum is very structured in that it presents specific activities in a particular sequence. In some cases you and I both will need to do some careful recording of your child's responses to certain procedures and activities. We will start by spending time just watching your child and carefully observing your child's responses to a variety of situations. We will begin by doing it together, then you can do it at home in your normal activities. I would also like to do some videotaping of your child. This will help us really focus on how he or she responds to certain situations. We will learn how he or she responds to specific sights, sounds, smells, touch, and movements.

It is very clear to me that you know your child better than anyone. But, through these observation activities, you may learn even more about your child. We can learn more about what your child enjoys most and what causes stress and discomfort. We will also learn more about the teaching strategies you are already using (some of which you may not even be aware you were doing!).

Next, we will focus on how to use systematic cues so that your child develops a better understanding of the world around him or her. An example of a cue might be letting your child smell the shampoo *every time* before you begin to wash his or her hair. We will also learn about subroutines (e.g., dressing using exactly the same sequence of steps, the same words, and touching him or her the same way each time). These strategies will help compensate for the areas he or she has trouble with, such as limited vision, hearing loss, extreme sensitivity to touch, or difficulty with movement. These strategies make it easier for your child to understand what is happening around him or her.

The last part of the curriculum focuses on helping your child be a more active participant in your interactions by developing turn-taking games. He or she will also learn to initiate more and to begin to develop certain communication skills. Although these communications won't necessarily be words, hopefully they will be clear and consistent.

Service providers should also read the Michael's Story case study and provide a copy to caregivers (see Appendixes D and E).

Important Questions

Before filling out the *Caregiver Interview*, the service provider should already know some of the answers to several key questions about the child's vision, hearing, motor skills, and overall health. This information should be found by using multiple data sources such as available reports, caregiver interviews, and consultation with other service providers and relevant professionals who have had previous experience with the child.

Vision

1. How does this child use his or her vision? How much time does the child need to respond to a visual stimulus? What does he or she like to look at? What does he or she seem to recognize visually?
2. When was the last time that this child had his or her eyes checked? Who did this examination?
3. Does this child have a visual impairment? If yes, what is the type and degree of vision loss?
4. Does this child wear corrective lenses? Who is the child's optometrist or ophthalmologist?
5. Is this child receiving services from a teacher credentialed in the area of visual impairment?

Hearing

1. How does this child use his or her hearing? How much time does the child need to respond to sound? What does he or she seem to listen to? What sounds does he or she seem to recognize? What words does he or she seem to understand?
2. When was the last time that this child had his or her hearing checked? Who did this evaluation?
3. Does this child have a hearing impairment? If yes, what is the type and degree of hearing loss?
4. Does this child wear hearing aids? Who is the audiologist?

Motor Skills

1. How does he or she grasp, hold, or handle toys and objects?
2. Is he or she sitting, standing, or walking without help?
3. Does this child have a motor disorder? If yes, what is it? Is it progressive?
4. Is there a physical therapist or occupational therapist involved with him or her?
5. Is this child receiving services from a teacher accredited in the area of hearing impairment?

Health

1. How would you describe the child's health?
2. If this child has medical problems, what are they?
3. Is this child taking any medication? If yes, what medication? What is it used to treat? Are there any side effects?

Summary

1. What are the child's main strengths?
2. In what situations does this child seem to be the most attentive and responsive?
3. What are this child's primary needs?
4. What current services is this child receiving?

Module 1

Understanding Your Child's Cues

RATIONALE

Because the communicative behaviors of children with multiple disabilities are often subtle and atypical, it is important for caregivers to become highly attuned to the child's behavioral repertoire and the meaning of his or her cues.

GOAL

After completing Module 1, caregivers will have a detailed picture of the ways in which the child expresses attention and interest in daily activities; internal states, such as pleasure and discomfort; and needs and desires.

DIRECTIONS TO THE SERVICE PROVIDER

1. Read Module 1 and become familiar with the main ideas.
2. Review each objective before you plan to introduce it to the caregiver. Practice how you will explain key concepts, and practice demonstrating how to complete relevant forms.
3. Duplicate handouts for Module 1 to give to the caregiver when you introduce each objective.
4. Introduce Module 1 to the caregiver by providing the overview handout (see also Appendixes D and E).

	Overview of Module 1: Understanding Your Child's Cues
Rationale	Children communicate in many ways, long before they begin to talk. When you respond and correctly interpret these early communications (e.g., facial expressions, sounds, pointing), it helps your child to understand language and encourages him or her to communicate even more. When children have multiple disabilities (e.g., severe developmental delays, hearing loss, visual impairment, difficulties with physical movement, or medical needs), their communication signals are often hard to recognize and understand. Before you can help your child to learn new ways of communicating, you must first discover the ways your child is currently communicating, as well as the kinds of things about which your child is most motivated to communicate.
Goal	The goal of Module 1 is to help you become a very careful observer of your child's *cues* (i.e., signals that communicate your child's feelings and desires). At the end of Module 1, you will have a very detailed picture of how your child expresses attention and interest, as well as what we call "state of arousal" (i.e., alert, sleepy, content, upset) and how he or she responds to changes in the environment.
Activities	Several activities have been designed to help you practice these observation skills and identify all the ways in which your child communicates. You will begin by taking a closer look at your child's daily activities. Through a series of careful observations focused on your child's typical day, you can keep track of his or her responses to the people and activities in the daily environment. Forms are provided to help you record communicative behaviors that can be difficult to recognize and might otherwise be easily overlooked.

OBJECTIVES AND PROCEDURES

After providing an overview of Module 1 (see above), introduce each objective. Each objective is listed here, followed by steps and examples. Blank forms for each example recording sheet are in Appendixes D and E.

Objective 1A

Typical Daily Schedule

▷ Caregivers will complete Recording Sheet 1-A: Typical Daily Activities, describing the child's typical day.

Recording Sheet 1-A

Date __5/11/00__   Child's name __Dante__   Observer's name __Mom__

Typical Daily Activities

Time	Activity	Likes	Dislikes	How do you know?
6–7 A.M.				
7–8 A.M.	I get Dante up.	✓		He gets excited and moves his arms.
8–9 A.M.	I feed him.		✓	He takes a long time, difficult to feed.
9–10 A.M.	I give him a bath.		✓	He squirms.
10–11 A.M.	PT on Monday, Teacher on Wednesday		✓	He fusses when they work with him.
11–12 P.M.				
12–1 P.M.				
1–2 P.M.				
2–3 P.M.				
3–4 P.M.				
4–5 P.M.				
5–6 P.M.				
6–7 P.M.				
7–8 P.M.				
8–9 P.M.				
9–10 P.M.				
10–11 P.M.				

Step 1

The week before introducing this module, ask the caregiver to think about the child's daily schedule or typical sequence of activities because you'll be asking questions about the daily routine during the next visit.

Step 2

The inventory of the child's day should be obtained by interviewing the caregiver. Using Recording Sheet 1-A: Typical Daily Activities (see Appendixes D and E), ask the caregiver to describe the typical sequence of activities in a typical day and describe:

- The activity and people involved
- Whether the child likes or dislikes the activity
- What the child does to convey preference or dislike

It is not necessary to fill in every time slot, as this is not intended to be a detailed daily log or inventory. Recording Sheet 1-A: Typical Daily Activities should be used simply to help caregivers think about the usual sequence of activities in their child's daily life. For some families this will be an easy task. For others, whose daily schedule is less structured or predictable, it may be more difficult. These families may be able to fill in only a few time slots with regularly occurring activities. The goal of this activity is *not* to document everything that occurs in a particular 24-hour period. Rather, the goals are

- To determine whether there are regularly occurring daily routines that are meaningful and/or pleasurable to the child
- To heighten the caregiver's awareness of the child's potential communicative behaviors
- To determine to what extent the family's daily routine includes predictable activities and situations

Step 3

If the child attends a center-based program, the teacher or the primary service provider should also complete an inventory reflecting the program's schedule from the time the child arrives until he or she departs.

Objective 1B

State of Arousal

Caregivers will learn to identify the child's state of arousal.

This objective has two parts. First, the service provider will help the caregiver observe and evaluate the child's state of arousal. It is important for parents to be able to recog-

Recording Sheet 1-B

Date **10/11/00**   Child's name **Kathie**   Observer's name **Dad**

Categories of States of Arousal

State	Description
Active and alert	Your child attempts to engage or interact with other people (e.g., looks at mother's face, vocalizes) or with the environment (e.g., reaches for a toy, bangs the table) using vision, hearing, sounds, or touch.
Crying or agitated	Your child vocalizes intensely, cries, or screams. Your child may grimace or frown with or without intense vocalization and may have increased body tension or intense movement.
Dazed or tuned out	Your child is awake but doesn't pay attention to sights, sounds, or touches. Your child's eyes may appear glassy or dull. He or she may move his or her limbs or body a little or startle slightly.
Drowsy	Your child's eyes are open but eyelids appear heavy; or your child's eyes may open and close repeatedly. He or she may vocalize.
Engaging in repetitive or stereotypical behavior	Your child is actively engaged in movements that are stereotypical, repetitive, or rhythmic (e.g., head weaving, waving arms, sucking or mouthing, rocking, hand flapping).
Fussy or irritable	Your child's sounds or facial expressions have a complaining or uncomfortable quality, but he or she is not yet crying.
Quiet and alert	Your child's eyes are open, and there is some focusing on sights, sounds, or touches. Your child may move his or her limbs or body a little or startle slightly.

How many of these states have you observed in your child?

State	When
Drowsy	After her massage
Irritable	In the bath
Quiet and alert	After the bouncing game

nize when the child who has severe disabilities is most likely to be able to attend to various sensations (e.g., sound, odor, touch, movement). Most often this will occur when the child is in a quiet alert state. Once the caregiver becomes familiar with the child's behavior in these various states, he or she can also more easily identify those behaviors of the child that signal preference or rejection, thus providing a more detailed understanding of the child's preferences for specific objects, people, and sensations. These observations should be made over a period of days, within naturally occurring situations, not all within a short space of time.

Step 1

Explain to the caregiver what is meant by *state*, that is the level and nature of the child's arousal and to what extent the child is able to attend to stimuli outside his or her own body. Use Recording Sheet I-B: Categories of States of Arousal for this discussion (see also Appendixes D and E). In most cases, a quiet alert state is optimal for allowing the child's energy and attention to be focused on the world around him or her. If the child is too drowsy, too agitated, too withdrawn, or too focused on repetitive self-stimulatory behavior, it will be more difficult for him or her to attend to and begin to make sense of his or her surrounding environment.

Step 2

Together with the caregiver, observe the child's behavior, and try to determine the child's state using the descriptions provided on Recording Sheet 1-B: Categories of States of Arousal. Discuss what it is about the child that leads you to this conclusion. Note observations in the section provided. If a videotape of the child is available, you and the caregiver can practice observing other states of arousal.

Note

The categories of states of arousal in newborns are based on the work of Brazelton (1984). Guess and his colleagues (1993) examined the states of arousal in children with profound and multiple disabilities. In our field testing, caregivers commented that they like learning about states of arousal because all infants demonstrate them and the categories gave them words to describe their child's behaviors.

Objective 1C

ABC Analysis

Through careful observation of events, behaviors, and consequences, caregivers will develop a clear understanding of the child's typical reactions to familiar routine events and activities.

This objective will provide an opportunity for caregivers to verify their impressions reflected in Recording Sheet 1-A: Typical Daily Activities and to develop a more detailed understanding of the meaning of their child's behavior.

Step 1

Explain the concepts of *antecedent, behavior,* and *consequence* to the caregiver by using the example shown in *Situations, Antecedents, Behaviors, and Consequences* (see also Appendixes D and E). The *behavior* is what the child actually does. Here are some typical behaviors:

- Grimaces
- Smiles
- Quiets; becomes still
- Opens hands; relaxes hands
- Extends fingers or toes
- Waves or swipes arms
- Moves arms and legs excitedly
- Turns head
- Vocalizes; cries
- Smiles; laughs
- Arches back; stiffens trunk
- Extends legs
- Opens mouth; protrudes tongue
- Chews on hands or fingers

The *antecedent* happens just before the child's behavior occurs, and the *consequence* is what happens immediately after the child's behavior, as shown in these examples.

Example 1

Mrs. U says, "time for your bottle," and holds the bottle to the baby's mouth (antecedent). Sophie kicks her feet (behavior). Mrs. U wiggles Sophie's toes and says, "Oh, you're hungry" (consequence). Herman, her 4-year-old son, turns the Barney song up to a very loud volume (antecedent). Sophie becomes still and begins to smile (behavior). Herman looks at Sophie, pats her arm, and says, "You like Barney" (consequence).

Example 2

At lunch time Mrs. J places Betty in the highchair. Betty begins banging the tray with both hands. Mrs. J says, "Hold on! I'm getting it as soon as I can!" The antecedent is Mrs. J's placing Betty in the highchair. Betty's behavior is banging the tray with both hands. The consequence of that behavior is Mrs. J's verbal response.

Step 2

Videotape the caregiver and the child in a familiar daily activity, such as mealtime and playtime for preschoolers or dressing and bath time for infants. Videotape review is essential for learning to identify antecedent events and consequences.

Situations, Antecedents, Behaviors, and Consequences

This chart can help you recognize antecedents, behaviors, and consequences with your own child. It can also help you fill out Recording Sheet 1-C. This example shows possible antecedents, behaviors, and consequences for bath time, an everyday activity. It is important to notice that a behavior is connected to what happens before it. Sometimes, if you change the antecedent, you can change the behavior.

Situation
(What is happening?)
Bath time

Antecedent (What happens just before the child's behavior?)	**Behavior** (What does the child do?)	**Consequence** (How does the caregiver respond to the child's behavior?)
Mom undresses Joey and puts him in the bath.	Joey arches his back and cries.	Mom changes his position.
Mom dips his toes in the water, then puts him in the bath.	Joey grimaces.	Mom talks to him.
Mom says, "Bath time!" and puts him in the bath.	Joey whimpers a little.	Mom soothes him.
Mom begins to wash Joey's face and hair.	Joey screams.	Mom sings to him.
Mom puts the shampoo bottle under Joey's nose.	Joey becomes quiet and alert.	Mom talks to him.

Understanding Your Child's Cues

Step 3

Watch the videotape with the caregiver, assisting the caregiver in carefully observing the child's and caregiver's behaviors described in Step 4, explaining and demonstrating the concepts of antecedent, behavior, and consequence. You both may have to watch the tape several times to develop a clear understanding of these concepts.

During this visit and after viewing the tape, practice observing the child's "live" response. For example, tickle the child's tummy (antecedent) and observe his or her response (behavior), or give the child a toy (antecedent) and observe the child's response (behavior). With the caregiver, record your observations on Recording Sheet I-C: Observations of Your Child's Responses to Daily Activities (see also Appendixes D and E).

Step 4

Using Recording Sheet I-C: Observations of Your Child's Responses to Daily Activities, ask the caregiver to observe the child in familiar, routine activities during the following week. Here are some examples:

- Awakening
- Dressing
- Brushing teeth
- Combing hair
- Applying lotion
- Massaging
- Therapy routines
- Mealtimes
- Bath time
- Nap time
- Bedtime
- Play routines
- Transporting (e.g., riding in stroller or wheelchair, riding in car)
- Caregiver reunion (e.g., mother returns)
- Greeting from familiar person (e.g., brother says "Hi")
- Other activities from Recording Sheet 1-A: Typical Daily Activities

Note

These observations can be made over a period of several days or all on one day. It is important for the caregiver not to feel overwhelmed by this assignment. Help the caregiver identify and select activities for observation. The number and variety of observations will depend on the individual caregiver. Suggest that several copies of Recording Sheet 1-C: Observations of Your Child's Responses to Daily Activities be placed in various locations in the home to make recording more convenient.

Recording Sheet 1-C

Child's name __June__   Observer's name __Mom__   Date __11/11/00__

Observations of Your Child's Responses to Daily Activities

First fill in the situation and behavior sections, then reflect on the antecedents and consequences of your child's behavior.

Situation (What is happening?)	Antecedent (What happens just before your child's behavior?)	Behavior (What does your child do?)	Consequence (How do you respond to your child's behavior?)
Breakfast	I put June in the highchair.	She bangs on the tray.	I talk to her.
Dressing	Dad puts her on the table.	She arches her back and cries.	Dad soothes her.
Getting her out of the crib	I pick her up.	She stiffens and whimpers.	I sing to her to relax her.

Step 5

In each situation, caregivers should be encouraged to describe the behavior and then note the antecedent (what happened just before the child's behavior) and the consequence (what happened following the behavior).

Objective 1D
Getting the Caregiver's Attention

Caregivers will identify and describe ways in which the child intentionally obtains the attention of the caregiver and for what purposes.

An important skill in the development of communication is learning to initiate an interaction by getting the caregiver's attention.

Step 1

Ask the caregiver whether and how the child intentionally gets the caregiver's attention throughout the day when the caregiver is busy with something else and not paying attention to the child. Ask the caregiver to record as many instances as noted over a period of several days on Recording Sheet I-D: Your Child's Strategies and Purposes for Getting Attention (see Appendixes D and E).

Step 2

Whenever possible, the caregiver should indicate what the child is trying to communicate in these situations (e.g., wants attention, is hungry, wants change of position or location).

Example 1

The infant is lying quietly in the crib. Mother is busy fixing breakfast for her older children, who are gathered in the kitchen. The infant begins to whine loudly and kick the side of the crib. The attention-getting behavior (initiation) is whining and kicking. Mother feels that the purpose is to join the others in the kitchen.

Note

For the young child with severe multiple disabilities and significant developmental delays, intentional attention-getting behavior may be very late to develop. Procedures for developing this ability are included in Module 5. The attention-getting behavior needs to be purposeful and not just automatic or reflexive. For example, if the child is simply crying because he's hungry, this is not really intentional attention-getting behavior. The child should be able to control these behaviors and use them to get the caregiver's attention whenever he or she wants.

Recording Sheet 1-D

Child's name ___Max___ Observer's name ___Dad___

Your Child's Strategies and Purposes for Getting Attention

Describe a situation in which your child was trying to get your attention.	How did your child get your attention?	What do you think your child was trying to communicate?	Date observed
Max is in his crib.	He makes a lot of noise.	"Come and pick me up."	6/30/00
I'm cooking lunch for Max, and he is sitting in his highchair.	He hits the tray.	"I want to eat."	7/02/00
We're watching TV, and Max is lying in his playpen beside the sofa.	He cries.	"Pick me up."	7/15/00

Objective 1E

Internal States and Feelings

Caregivers will describe how the child reacts to internal states and expresses feelings.

Step 1

Ask caregivers to refer to the initial interview in which they were asked similar questions about their child's communicative behavior. This activity provides an opportunity to look back at their responses and reflect on how the child's behavior may have changed. In addition, by this point in using the curriculum, many caregivers will have become much keener observers of their child's behavior and may have new understanding of the communicative value of certain behaviors.

Step 2

Ask caregivers whether there are any changes in their original perceptions of their child's expression of internal states. This procedure differs from previous objectives because the child's experience is not under the control of the caregiver. Thus, the caregiver's judgments regarding the child's reactions to internal states are necessarily speculative. Examples of the child's expressions of internal states may include

- Hunger
- Discomfort (e.g. wet, soiled); pain (e.g., gas)
- Fatigue
- Pleasure; happiness
- Fear
- Surprise
- Boredom
- Overstimulation

After using the strategies described in Module 1, encourage the caregiver to record the child's behaviors by completing the module summary of accomplishments (see Appendixes D and E). This information may be shared with other caregivers or service providers.

Module 2

Identifying Your Child's Preferences

RATIONALE

The key to all learning is motivation. One of the best ways to encourage a child with multiple disabilities to communicate is to identify those things that are most interesting and important to him or her. These will be the objects, people, and activities about which the infant is most likely to communicate. The careful observations outlined in Module 1 should make it possible to generate a detailed description of the child's most and least preferred items.

GOAL

Caregivers will develop a thorough understanding of what the child enjoys and what he or she dislikes.

DIRECTIONS TO THE SERVICE PROVIDER

1. Read Module 2 and become familiar with the main ideas.
2. Review each objective before you plan to introduce it to the caregiver. Practice how you will explain key concepts and how you will demonstrate how to complete relevant forms.
3. Duplicate handouts for Module 2 to give to the caregiver when you introduce each objective.
4. Introduce Module 2 to the caregiver by providing the overview handout (see also Appendixes D and E).

	Overview of Module 2: Identifying Your Child's Preferences
Rationale	Motivation is the key to any kind of learning. Knowing your child's likes and dislikes for different objects, people, foods, and activities is very useful. Your child's likes and dislikes can be used in motivating him or her to communicate to obtain or reject these things. Now that you have completed the observations in Module 1, it is simple to identify your child's least and most favorite things. Later, in Module 4, you will learn some simple strategies for using these things to teach your child new ways to communicate.
Goal	The goal of Module 2 is to develop a list of preferences. This list will need to be updated periodically over time because preferences will change as your child matures.
Activities	The activities for Module 2 are simple. You will list the people, objects, and activities that your child likes, identifying which of those he or she especially loves and which of those he or she really hates! You will take a careful look at your child's responses to certain people, objects, and activities when they are presented and when they are removed.

OBJECTIVES AND PROCEDURES

After providing an overview of Module 2 (see above), introduce each objective. Each objective is listed here, followed by steps and examples. Blank forms for each example recording sheet are available in Appendixes D and E.

Objective 2A

High and Low Preference

Caregivers will generate a detailed list of activities, people, and objects that they believe their child enjoys and those that the child particularly dislikes.

Step 1

Using information gathered for the second and fourth objectives in Module 1, as well as information obtained in the initial caregiver interview, list the child's high and low preferences on Recording Sheet 2-A: Your Child's Preferences (see Appendixes D and E).

Recording Sheet 2-A

Child's name __Jenny__ Observer's name __Mom__ Date __12/12/00__

Your Child's Preferences

	Really Likes	Likes	Dislikes	Really Dislikes
People				
Brother	✓			
Mother		✓		
Doctor				✓
Objects				
Caterpillar	✓			
Kooshball				✓
Rattle		✓		
Activities				
Bouncing on the ball		✓		
Bath time			✓	
Swinging	✓			

Step 2

Using the information in Recording Sheet 1-A: Typical Daily Activities, ask caregivers to add to the list any additional things the child likes and dislikes during each of those times.

Step 3

Mark each of these high- and low-preference items in terms of the relative intensity of the preference or dislike on Recording Sheet 2-A. For example, if the child has an intense desire or preference for yogurt, it should be marked in the "Really Likes" column. If he or she also likes being rocked but the level of his enjoyment and enthusiasm is somewhat less than for eating yogurt, mark the "Likes" column. For disliked items, if the child intensely dislikes having his or her face washed, mark the "Really Dislikes" column. If he or she dislikes loud music but is somewhat inconsistent in his response or shows only moderate irritation, mark the "Dislikes" column, and so on. For some young children, it may not be possible to differentiate between loves and likes or hates and dislikes.

Objective 2B

Presentation and Removal

Caregivers will learn to describe the child's reaction to the presentation and removal of familiar and unfamiliar objects and events.

For this objective, observations will be made of the child's behaviors in structured situations. Unlike most procedures in this curriculum, this one is somewhat contrived. It can sometimes be better understood if you describe it as a "game" in which all family members can participate.

Step 1

Explain to the caregiver that a key to encouraging the child's communication and interaction is to have a clear understanding not only of the child's behaviors and states but also of what is most interesting and motivating to him or her. These might be activities or events (e.g., hearing a favorite record), certain people or animals (e.g., grandmother or the family's dog), foods (e.g., applesauce), or certain objects (e.g., a favorite toy or a pacifier). It is also important to know what the child strongly dislikes.

Step 2

Ask the caregiver to present a favorite object (e.g., music box) or activity (e.g., singing) while you observe. Record the child's reactions on Recording Sheet 2-B: Your Child's Responses to People, Objects, and Activities. Ask the caregiver to remove the object or stop the activity. Then try an unfamiliar object or activity. Record the child's responses

Recording Sheet 2-B

Date **9/11/00**   Child's name **Matt**   Observer's name **Mom**

Your Child's Responses to People, Objects, and Activities

Before filling this out, refer to Recording Sheet 1-B for descriptions of states. Note that it is not necessary to present and take away each person, object, or event. Review your completed sheet to identify 1) differences in your child's responses in different states, 2) differences in your child's reactions to familiar and new experiences, 3) differences in your child's responses to removal and presentation, 4) what your child likes and dislikes, and 5) how your child demonstrates these likes and dislikes.

N = a new person, object, or event   F = a familiar person, object, or event

State	What did you present?	How did your child respond to this?	N	F
Fussy	I gave him a bottle.	He sucked.	✓	
Quiet/Alert	I dangled plastic keys.	He grasped them.	✓	
Fussy	Bouncing on a large ball	He cried and laid on the ball.	✓	
Quiet/Alert	Massage after bath	He relaxed and smiled.		✓

State	What did you take away?	How did your child respond to this?	N	F
Drowsy	His bottle	He cried.		✓
Active/Alert	Keys	No response	✓	
Crying	Stopped bouncing the ball	He quieted and smiled.	✓	
Alert	Stopped massage	He seemed sleepy.		✓

30   *PLAI* Module 2

on Recording Sheet 2-B. Practice these observations several times during your visit with the caregiver. Show the caregiver how you recorded these observations on the sheet.

Step 3

Using a blank Recording Sheet 2-B: Your Child's Responses to People, Objects, and Activities (see Appendixes D and E), ask the caregiver to make the following observations as many times as is convenient throughout the following week:

1. Note the child's state of arousal before beginning the presentation and removal procedure described below (refer to Objective 1-B in Module 1).

Example 1

Mrs. M decides to observe her infant Rosalie's reaction to a variety of foods at dinnertime. Before beginning the presentation of various foods, Mrs. M notes that Rosalie is somewhat drowsy and not particularly focused on dinner.

2. Present or remove object or event. Wait quietly without providing other prompts for at least 10 or 15 seconds.

3. Describe what happens. That is, describe the circumstances around the presentation of the object or event. For example, if a new toy is presented, what are the accompanying cues? Is the toy placed in the child's hand? Does the caregiver say something to the child? Does the toy make a noise, move, or light up? Or, if someone walks into the room, does he or she speak to the child? Touch the child? Pick him or her up?

4. Record the child's responses.

Carefully record the child's response to the presentation of a variety of stimuli, including people (e.g., family members, peers, teachers), objects (e.g., foods, musical toy, spoon, blanket), and events (e.g., turning on TV or music, the scent of cologne, unpleasant aromas, calling the child's name, putting lotion on the child's arm, or swinging the child in a blanket). Note whether the child was familiar with the object, person, or activity or whether this was a new experience.

Example 2

Mrs. M begins by presenting a spoonful of chocolate pudding—a new food for Rosalie. She clinks the spoon gently on the bowl, scoops a spoon of pudding, and brings the spoon near Rosalie's nose and mouth, allowing her to smell the pudding. Then Mrs. M gives her a taste. She notes that Rosalie seems to become more alert, bobbing her head slightly, and she swallows the pudding quickly and easily. Next, noting that Rosalie is now more alert, Mrs. M picks up a glass of juice and says, "How about some juice?" She gives Rosalie a drink. Rosalie extends her head and arms and becomes somewhat agitated.

In the first presentation, Rosalie's state was drowsy. The object presented was pudding, a new experience. Rosalie's response to the presentation was to bob her head, swallow, and become more alert. During the second presentation, Rosalie's state was quiet and alert. The food, juice, was familiar. Rosalie's response to the presentation was to extend her head and arms, and she appeared agitated.

Record the child's response to the removal of objects (e.g., take away the toy that the child is grasping), people (e.g., leave the room yourself or have some other familiar person leave the room), or sensory stimuli (e.g., turn off the TV or radio), or delay of an expected event (e.g., wait a few seconds before giving the next bite of food).

Note

Explain to caregivers that although many times children may not respond to the presentation of an object or event, they may respond to the removal of an object or the delay of an expected event. Encourage the caregiver to provide ample time for the child to respond to the presentation or removal of the object. As will become clear in later modules, providing enough time for the child to respond is an important strategy in encouraging early communication.

Example 3

Mrs. M returns to the pudding, noting that Rosalie is now fairly calm and alert. Mrs. M just touches the spoon to Rosalie's lips giving her a very small taste, then withdraws the spoon. She waits 15 seconds. Rosalie begins to kick her legs on her highchair and opens and closes her hands. For this presentation, Rosalie's state was quiet and alert. The object that was presented was pudding. Her response to delay was to kick her highchair and open and close her hands.

Example 4

Mr. P notices his daughter Jenny is in a fussy state. He approaches her and turns on the tape player and places it near her. The tape is the Barney song that Jenny has heard many times. Mr. P observes Jenny's response to this event. Jenny stops fussing and becomes very quiet and still. Although she does not move or orient toward the sound in any way, she does appear to be listening to it. After about 3 minutes, the father turns off the tape. Jenny begins to flap her arms and brings her hand to her mouth and begins to chew her hand. Her initial state was fussy. The activity was listening to the Barney tape, which was familiar. Jenny's response to the presentation was to become quiet and still. Her response to removal of the tape was to flap her arms and chew her hand.

Step 3

In the next session, review the Recording Sheet 2-B: Your Child's Responses to People, Objects, and Activities that the caregiver has completed since your last visit, and discuss interesting patterns of responses to certain items. Also, ask the caregiver to think about whether and how the child's state seemed to affect the child's response to the various items and activities.

Note

Let the caregivers know that it is not necessary to present and take away every object, person, and event in completing this objective. Completion of this form provides an opportunity for service providers and caregivers to review the following:

1. *Differences in the child's responses in different states*
2. *Differences in the child's reactions to familiar versus new experiences*
3. *Differences in the child's responses to removal and presentation*
4. *Information about what the child likes and dislikes*
5. *Information about how the child demonstrates these likes and dislikes*

After using the strategies described in Module 2, encourage the caregiver to record the child's behaviors by completing the module summary of accomplishments (see Appendixes D and E). This information may be shared with other caregivers or service providers.

Module 3

Establishing Predictable Routines

RATIONALE

Modules 1 and 2 focused on the importance of motivation in early learning. Module 3 addresses the use of predictable routines as very important in supporting learning in children with severe and multiple disabilities. The establishment of predictable routines throughout the child's day has many benefits. First, the child will develop a sense of confidence and control over his or her environment by "knowing" what is about to happen and by being able to associate certain activities, people, and objects with cues that occur just prior to the event.

Predictable sequences, or *subroutines*, within familiar activities are also important. For example, the process of taking a bath may include sequences that occur each time. Such subroutines also assist the child with severe disabilities in understanding the world around him or her.

Once predictable activities and subroutines are identified or established, the consistent pairing of certain words, sights, and touch sensations with anticipated activities or objects will eventually give meaning to those cues. Consistent use of these cues can also help the child increase his or her attentional focus on key elements of the environment and eventually will make it easier for the caregiver and the child to establish joint attention to the same object or activity.

GOAL

Caregivers will create a daily routine that includes several predictable events that the child can anticipate and through recognition of certain cues such as sounds, sights, and other sensations.

DIRECTIONS TO THE SERVICE PROVIDER

1. Read Module 3 and become familiar with the main ideas.
2. Review each objective before you plan to introduce it to the caregiver. Practice how you will explain key concepts and how you will demonstrate how to complete relevant forms.
3. Duplicate handouts for Module 3 to give to the caregiver when you introduce each objective.
4. Introduce Module 3 to the caregiver by providing the overview handout (see also Appendixes D and E).

OBJECTIVES AND PROCEDURES

After providing an overview of Module 3 (see next page), introduce each objective. Each objective is listed here, followed by steps and examples. Blank forms for each example recording sheet are in Appendixes D and E.

Objective 3A

Creating a Predictable Daily Schedule

Caregivers will create a predictable daily routine by identifying at least five daily activities with the child that can be scheduled in the same sequence each day.

Step 1

Explain to caregivers that by scheduling certain events of the day at about the same time and in the same sequence (e.g., every day after breakfast the mother gives the child a bath), the child can more easily understand and learn about his or her environment. In addition, the child will begin to develop expectations and anticipation for certain activities.

Note

If an activity is pleasurable (e.g., the child enjoys a daily massage every day after her or his bath) and predictable, that activity can be delayed slightly and the child can eventually learn to request the activity through some communicative behavior (e.g., the child learns to vocalize after her or his bath; mother lets her or him feel the lotion bottle, then waits for her or him to request her or his daily massage). This procedure is discussed further in Modules 4 and 5.

	Overview of Module 3: Establishing Predictable Routines
Rationale	One of the things that helps children understand the world around them is having a predictable schedule. By identifying frequently occurring activities and establishing a consistent order in which they will occur each day, you can create for your child a sense of confidence and control over his or her environment. Your child will begin to understand what is about to happen by recognizing certain cues and signals that occur just prior to the familiar activity or event (e.g., getting undressed and playing Pat-a-cake before taking a bath). *Subroutines* are also important. These are consistent sequences or steps that occur within a familiar activity like bath time or dressing. Once these routines are established, the consistent pairing of certain words, sights, and touch sensations with each activity (e.g., always helping your child feel the running water before placing him or her in the bathtub) will eventually give meaning to those words or other cues. Making the most of your child's senses will increase his or her ability to anticipate familiar activities and daily events. Consistent use of these cues will also help your child increase his or her attentional focus and eventually will make it easier for you and your child to establish joint attention to a single object or activity.
Goal	There are three goals in Module 3. The first is to establish certain predictable events within your daily schedule (e.g., always rocking your child after lunch and before naptime). The second is to identify or establish certain subroutines within frequently occurring activities (e.g., always following the same steps and using the same words when changing your child's diaper). The third goal is to make maximum use of your child's senses to help him or her anticipate and understand these predictable events (e.g., always touching the back of his or her hand with the washcloth before washing his or her face).
Activities	Using Recording Sheet 1-A: Typical Daily Activities, you will identify the most predictable events in your daily routine. You may wish to increase the predictability of your daily schedule. You will also describe the specific steps of any existing subroutines that you use. Or you may wish to create one or two new subroutines that you think might be fun for both you and your child. In this module, you also may work on identifying ways of making greater use of your child's senses to help him or her anticipate and understand an activity.

Step 2

Ask the caregiver to identify five daily events or activities that occur fairly regularly. Review Recording Sheet 1-A: Typical Daily Activities (in Module 1) for examples of such events. Examples of five predictable events:

1. When the child wakes in the morning, the mother gives him or her cereal.
2. After cereal, the mother and sister give the child a bath.
3. After lunch, the mother watches television, and the child sits in an adaptive chair.
4. After dinner, the older sister rocks the child in a rocking chair.
5. After rocking, the mother changes the child and puts him or her on the sofa.

Step 3

During the next week, the caregiver can use Recording Sheet 3-A: Predictable Daily Activities (see Appendixes D and E) to identify the approximate time of the activity and what usually happens just before and just after each activity.

Example 1

One daily event that is quite consistent in Ms. R's home is watching the daily soaps. She reports that her child, Enrico, is usually on the floor on a blanket near the television during this time. This is usually a fairly calm time and one that Ms. R enjoys. As she observes during the week, she notes that usually just prior to this she changes Enrico's diaper, spreads the blanket on the floor, and places Enrico on his stomach. She gets herself a cup of coffee and sits on the couch. When the television shows are over, she often calls a friend unless Enrico is fussy. If he is fussy, she prepares a bottle and tries to get him to take a nap. Another consistent activity for Ms. R is cooking dinner for herself and her brother. Her brother almost always comes to her apartment after work and eats with her and Enrico. Again, after observing during the week, she realizes that sometimes as she begins to fix dinner, she turns on the radio. Sometimes Enrico is awake in his crib in the bedroom, sometimes he is in his highchair, and sometimes he is on a blanket in the living room.

Predictable Events in Enrico's Daily Schedule

8–9 A.M.:	Enrico wakes up
9–10 A.M.:	Breakfast
10–11 A.M.:	Bath
11–1 P.M.:	Variable
1–3 P.M.:	Mom watches television shows; Enrico lays on blanket
3–4 P.M.:	Nap
4–6 P.M.:	Variable
6–7 P.M.:	Mom fixes dinner
7–10 P.M.:	Variable
10–11 P.M.:	Bed time

In this example of Enrico's day, the routine of laying Enrico on the blanket and turning on the television was very predictable. The second event, fixing dinner, was a regularly occurring activity for Ms. R, but the experience for Enrico was somewhat variable. The service provider could suggest to Ms. R that, whenever possible, Enrico be placed in the infant seat in the kitchen when she starts to fix dinner. Also, it could be suggested that she always turn on the radio as she starts to cook. This would increase the number of cues (i.e., being placed in the infant seat, hearing the radio, and smelling the food) available to Enrico to help him understand that dinner is imminent.

Recording Sheet 3-A

Child's name __Sam__   Observer's name __Mom__

Predictable Daily Activities

First fill in the daily activity, then note the approximate time and what happens before and after the activity.

What usually happens before?	Daily activity	Approximate time	What usually happens after?
Breakfast	Bath	11 AM	I dress him, then it depends.
Depends on the day	Nap time	2 PM	His brother plays with him.

Step 4

At your next visit with the caregiver, determine whether it is possible to maintain the sequence of the five activities on a daily basis.

Step 5

Assist the caregiver in making a daily schedule using either Recording Sheet 1-A: Typical Daily Schedule or Recording Sheet 3-A: Predictable Daily Activities (see Appendixes D and E). It is important to convey to caregivers that the intent here is simply to incorporate several predictable routines in the daily schedule. Families need not completely reconstruct their lives according to some rigid time schedule. If the accepted schedule does not really fit the family's lifestyle, it should be modified until it is fairly predictable yet comfortable for the family.

Step 6

If the family has few predictable activities in the daily schedule, the goal will be to increase the predictability of the day by gradually including at least five regularly occurring events. Work on these one at a time. Do not try to add a second predictable activity until the family is comfortable with the first one, and so on.

Note

For some families this will not be an easy goal. Much trial and error may be required to come up with activities that can be consistently scheduled. It is important that the interventionist avoid giving the message that a lifestyle that is flexible and spontaneous is bad. Rather, help parents understand that because of the child's reduced access to meaningful sensory information, it is necessary to create meaning for the child through repetition and predictability.

Objective 3B

Identifying Subroutines

Caregivers will identify predictable sequences within specific activities, or *subroutines*.

In addition to the predictable daily routine, it can also be very helpful to have smaller predictable sequences within the activities that occur frequently as part of the daily schedule. These routines are referred to as *subroutines*. They are small routines that occur within the larger routine of the daily schedule. For example, within the daily routine of giving the child a bath, then rocking her, then putting her to bed, the bath time may include a consistent sequence. This would be a subroutine.

Recording Sheet 3-B

Child's name __Joey__   Observer's name __Dad__

Subroutines and Cues

Use a separate recording sheet for each activity.

Activity
Bath time

Subroutine	Cues I usually use	New cues to add
Put Joey in the tub.	I show him the bathtub.	Put Joey's hand in the water.
Wash him with a sponge.	None	Help him squeeze the sponge.
Shampoo his hair.	None	Have him smell the shampoo.
Take him out and dry him off.	I pick him up.	Tap under his elbows.

Step 1

Help families understand subroutines by giving them several examples. If possible, provide videotaped examples of such routines and, together with the caregiver, practice analyzing the sequence of events within the subroutine. Explain that in all families there will be certain activities that are engaged in frequently (e.g., mealtimes, playing Pat-a-Cake, dressing, singing a song). Often such activities are *routinized*, that is, they follow a familiar script and sequence. For example, when Mrs. S dresses Joey, who has severe physical disabilities, she generally follows this routine:

- Lays Joey on his back on the bed
- Slips on Joey's pants
- Sits him up, saying "Up we go."
- Pulls a shirt over his head, saying "Where's Joey?"
- Guides his left arm in, then guides his right arm in
- Pulls his shirt down saying, "Cover up that tummy."
- Rubs Joey's tummy, then picks him up

Step 2

Ask caregivers to try over the next week to identify activities that occur fairly often (even if they do not always occur at the same time) and list them on Recording Sheet 3-B: Subroutines and Cues (see Appendixes D and E). Examples might be playing a favorite music tape, reading a book, going for a walk in the stroller, sitting in the backyard, eating ice cream, and so on.

Step 3

Next, ask caregivers to try to determine which of these activities include predictable subroutines. Using Recording Sheet 3-B again, list the elements of each subroutine.

Step 4

For activities that occur frequently but do not include predictable subroutines, encourage caregivers to design subroutines.

Example 1

Although Mrs. V always fixes breakfast for Donella soon after she gets up, the activity includes very little consistency. So, Mrs. V planned the following sequence or subroutine:

- After changing Donella's diapers, say to her, "Time for breakfast."
- Carry her to the kitchen.
- Set Donella in the highchair.
- Get Donella's bib and say, "Here's your bib."
- Put the bib on Donella.
- Mix up the cereal.

- Carry the cereal bowl and spoon to her tray, and sit down next to her.
- Say, "Here's your cereal, Donella."
- Feed Donella her cereal.

See Example 2 in the following objective to see how additional cues are added to this sequence.

Objective 3C

Adding Cues

Caregivers will identify specific auditory, visual, tactile, olfactory, and kinesthetic cues that can be used to help their child anticipate familiar activities and daily situations.

Note

Infants with multiple disabilities often have difficulty receiving information through more typical modes such as the sound of spoken words or the sight of familiar surroundings and activities. Thus, it is necessary to provide plenty of information carefully through those senses that are available to the child, such as the senses of touch and movement, smell, and whatever hearing or vision the child has available.

Step 1

Explain to caregivers the benefits of providing specific cues to help children anticipate and understand familiar activities and events. Cues may be added to a subroutine or to the daily schedule to mark predictable events.

Step 2

Help the caregiver identify specific cues that can be used consistently to help the infant anticipate the activity.

Note

Cues that are easy and convenient to make are more likely to be used by the caregiver. Cues that have an obvious relationship to the referent are more likely to be understood by the child. Selected cues must be accessible to the child, that is, a child who is totally blind cannot use visual cues, and a child who is profoundly deaf will not hear sound cues. Also, cues must be either pleasant or neutral for the child. Cues that are unpleasant or overstimulating should not be used. Descriptions of auditory, visual, tactile, kinesthetic, and olfactory cues are provided on the following pages and in Appendixes D and E.

If the child has a hearing loss, service providers and families should consult with an audiologist and teacher certified in the area of hearing loss regarding the child's type and

Tactile Cues

Tactile cues involve touching your child in a specific way to let him or her know what is about to happen. They are very helpful for communicating with young children who have severe physical disabilities and developmental delays or severe visual impairments and hearing loss.

Touch cues should be precise, perceivable, and pleasant for the child in order to support attention and anticipation of an activity. Use one touch cue at a time. It will be more difficult for a child with severe disabilities to learn the exact meaning of a touch cue if more than one touch cue is used in a single activity or if the cue occurs simultaneously with touching the child during physical handling and interaction. Certain types of touch on specific body areas may elicit reflex movements in some children with motor or neurological impairments.

Other young children with medical needs dislike being touched on the bottom of the foot because of their experience with medical interventions. In general, a firm or deep pressure touch is more easily tolerated than a light, feathery stroke. However, the type of touch and placement of each touch cue should be selected carefully for the individual child, then used systematically.

Here are some touch cues that may work for your child:

- Before washing your child's face, stroke his or her cheek.
- Before giving your child a drink from a cup, hold his or her chin.
- Tap your child's lips twice with your fingers before giving him or her the first bite of food.

Here is a manual cue that may work for your child:

- Before giving your child a bite of food, physically guide him or her to sign the word EAT (i.e., sign together).

Here are some object cues that may work for your child:

- Touch the washcloth to your child's hand before putting him or her into the bath tub.
- When dressing your child, touch the shirt to your child's chest before putting it on him or her.

Auditory Cues

Sound cues are a natural way to get a child's attention. At first, most children tend to be more responsive to rhythmic sound or exaggerated intonation.

In order for the child to make use of sounds as meaningful cues, background noise (i.e., television, radio, and other distracting environmental sounds) should be eliminated as much as possible so that the child can focus on the auditory cues.

Some kinds of sounds may be irritating to a particular child. For example, some children with disabilities are extremely sensitive and may overreact to any increase in loudness. Also, sudden bursts of sound may cause a child to startle and even cry. Some environments cause sound reverberation that may be irritating and may make it more difficult for the child who has hearing loss or auditory processing disorder to attend to and localize specific sounds. Generally, this occurs in rooms with little sound-absorbing material. For example, a kitchen with a tile floor and no curtains would be a much more resonant noise environment than a living room with carpet, curtains, and overstuffed furniture. Many children who have a hearing loss have some residual hearing and can perceive some sounds.

Here are some sound cues that may work for your child:

- Clink the spoon on the side of the bowl before giving your child a bite.
- Gently tap the cup on the table before giving your child a drink.
- Sing a few lines of the theme song of your child's favorite television show before turning on the television.
- Shake your child's bottle of milk near his or her head before putting the nipple to his or her mouth.

Here are some word cues that may work for your child:

- Say your child's name when you are about to present something to him or her, when you are about to interact with him or her, or when you are about to greet him or her.
- In simple language, tell your child what you are about to do (e.g., "Mama's going to wash your face now.").
- Use single key words as cues (e.g., "wash," "dinner").

Kinesthetic Cues

Kinesthetic or movement cues are actually combinations of movement and tactile sensation. They involve handling, positioning, and moving your child in certain ways associated with the upcoming activity. If a child has cerebral palsy, kinesthetic cues should be selected with consideration for the child's muscle tone. Children with low tone (hypotonia) tend to mold easily when held but may be difficult to arouse. They usually benefit from physical stimulation, handling, and positioning that increase muscle tone and arouse attention. Children with high tone (hypertonia) may be irritable and difficult to hold. Specific positioning and careful handling will be needed to reduce tone and improve the quality, amount, and range of the child's movements. Do not use kinesthetic cues that elicit reflexive or involuntary movements (e.g., if turning the child's head to one side causes the child's legs and arms to move in the same direction or if swinging the child without proper positioning and support triggers trunk and limb extension). In general, hold and support your child while moving him or her so that he or she can maintain a symmetrical and flexed body position.

Here are some whole body movement cues that may work for your child:

- Before sitting down to rock your child in a rocking chair, rock back and forth while holding him or her at your shoulder.
- Hold your child away from your body, and gently swing him or her before putting your child in an infant swing.

Here are some limb movement cues that may work for your child:

- Before lifting your child out of the highchair, lift up slightly on his or her elbows.
- Lift your child's arms above his or her head before taking his or her shirt off.
- Clap your child's hands together once before playing Pat-a-cake.

Olfactory Cues

Smells associated with objects and people can be used as olfactory cues. Your child may anticipate that you are going to pick him or her up if you always wear the same cologne. Some children may be very sensitive to certain smells, yet other children may not seem to notice them. Carefully observe your child's preferences and responses to smells. Some children are extremely sensitive to cologne and other strong odors. You will need to observe carefully to determine whether certain odors produce overstimulation or a negative reaction from your child.

Here are some smell cues that may work for your child:

- Before washing your child's hair, let him or her smell the shampoo.
- Let your child smell the food in the bowl before giving him or her the first bite.
- Make it a habit to wear the same cologne on your wrists. Before picking up your child, hold your wrist close to his or her nose, then greet your child.

Visual Cues

The use of color, contrast, lighting, spacing, and arrangement can make an object more visible to children with severe disabilities. Objects can be seen more easily when they are against a solid, glare-free background of contrasting color. For example, a white bowl on a blue place mat has better contrast than a white bowl on a white highchair tray. The human face is a low-contrast visual image, so a child with visual impairment may have difficulty recognizing his or her dark-skinned, brown-haired mother who is wearing a tan blouse and is sitting in front of a wall of wood paneling. Contrast can be used to make the mother's face easier to see: The mother might put on bright lipstick, wear a blue blouse, or sit in front of a white wall.

Distracting visual objects should be reduced so that your child's visual attention can be engaged. For example, some children may be distracted from the activity if they face an open window with bright sunshine, or they will have difficulty seeing an object that is placed among other toys or on a patterned quilt. Visual cues should be presented within the child's visual field, and the child should be encouraged to look at and (when appropriate) touch the object. Systematic and consistent use of color, lighting, and contrast can assist your child in organizing visual information and in recognizing familiar situations.

Here is a lighting cue that may work for your child:

- Before beginning a familiar activity, use a flashlight in a dimly lit area to focus your child's attention on a specific object that will be used first in the activity (e.g., highlight a favorite toy, cup, or your face).

Here are some contrast cues that may work for your child:

- Before placing your child in the highchair, place a brightly colored bowl on the highchair, to signal mealtime.
- Before placing your child on the floor, place a colorful favorite toy on a different colored quilt to indicate playtime.

Here is a color cue that may work for your child:

- Select objects in black, white, and primary colors to use as cues for daily activities (e.g., use a blue washcloth to indicate bath time, or select a yellow bottle or red cup for your child's milk.

Here is a manual cue that may work for your child:

- Use a conventional gesture or key word sign (if appropriate) to signal an activity. Make these hand movements slowly, and repeat them. Wear a solid, high contrast shirt to make your hands easy to see.

degree of hearing loss, use of hearing aids, and strategies to provide the child with access to sound cues and other auditory information. If the child has a visual impairment, service providers and families should consult the child's ophthalmologist or optometrist and a teacher certified in the area of visual impairments to obtain information about the child's type and degree of vision loss and strategies for improving the child's access to visual cues and visual information. If the child has motor or neurological impairments, service providers and families should consult the child's physical or occupational therapist in selecting touch cues, kinesthetic cues, and olfactory cues and for deciding how to provide them to this child.

Consistent pairing of a cue and an event is essential in helping the child to understand the meaning of the cue. For example, if mother consistently says, "It's bath time" close to the child's ear, while rubbing the child's arm with a dry washcloth, eventually the child may associate whatever auditory cues he or she can perceive, and the feeling of the washcloth with bath time. Thus, he or she understands the cues.

Several cues may be combined and used sequentially or simultaneously. For example, the caregiver may say, "Here's your bottle" while touching the baby's cheek with the nipple, or the caregiver may touch the baby's cheek and then say, "Here's your bottle." There is no single correct way to use anticipatory cues. Consistency is the key. It will be difficult for an infant to develop anticipation of getting a bottle if sometimes his cheek is touched and other times his lips are tapped or his chin is stroked. In some cases, multimodal cues may be overstimulating or confusing for a child; however, this can really only be determined by trial and error and careful observation. In such cases, only one cue should be used at a time.

Step 3

Help the caregiver identify cues that already occur naturally, at least occasionally. These existing cues will be easier for the caregiver to incorporate on a regular basis. Use Recording Sheet 3-B: Subroutines and Cues (see Appendixes D and E) to note cues that are usually used and new cues that will be added.

Example 1

Mr. L noticed that often when he picked up his son, Angelo, out of his wheelchair, the boy would startle and begin to fuss. He also noticed, however, that sometimes this did not occur. More careful observation revealed that if Mr. L spoke to Angelo before picking him up and touched him gently on the arm, Angelo was less likely to become upset. Mr. L decided to try always saying, "Angelo, I'm gonna pick you up now," followed by lifting up slightly on Angelo's arms.

Example 2

The following example shows how Mrs. V (from the example in Step 4 of Identifying Subroutines) added various cues (marked by italics) to Donella's breakfast subroutine.

1. After changing Donella's diapers, say to her, "Time for breakfast."
2. *Bring Donella's hand to her own lips.*
3. Carry her to the kitchen.

4. *Place Donella's hand on the tray of the highchair.*
5. Set Donella in the highchair.
6. Get Donella's bib.
7. *Help her touch the bib and say, "Here's your bib."*
8. *Touch her chest, then put the bib on Donella.*
9. Mix up the cereal.
10. Carry cereal bowl and spoon to her tray, and sit down next to her.
11. *Bang the spoon on the bowl lightly.*
12. Say, "Here's your cereal, Donella."
13. *Touch the edge of the spoon to Donella's mouth.*
14. Wait for Donella to open her mouth.
15. Begin feeding her cereal.
16. *When finished with feeding, touch the washcloth to Donella's hand, then wipe her face, saying, "All done!"*

Step 4

Stress to the caregiver that such cues may not be helpful unless they are used fairly consistently and frequently. Also whenever possible, caregivers should wait until the child is in a quiet, alert state before presenting the cues. Although this is not always necessary or convenient, if the child is in an alert state, he or she is more likely to be aware of the cues and to learn to associate them with the activity that follows. The caregiver may note the child's responses to cues on Recording Sheet 3-C: Effectiveness of New Cues.

Step 5

Once the cues have been used consistently for 1 or 2 weeks, caregivers may want to try pausing a few seconds following the cue. This will provide an opportunity to observe the child's behavior for evidence of whether he or she seems to be focusing attention and anticipating the event. If so, then a simple time delay procedure (described in Module 5) can be used to encourage the child to communicate a request for the activity. It is difficult to predict how long it may take for the child to begin to anticipate an activity. First, the child must learn to associate the cue with a specific activity. This will depend on several factors, for example, the consistency and frequency of the cues and the motivational strength of the activity. For example, a child may learn to associate cues related to eating ice cream—his favorite food—much faster than the cues associated with being put down for a nap. Although a child may learn to anticipate one activity in 2 weeks, it may take months to learn to anticipate another activity.

Example 3

Mr. L and his wife both consistently used the cues described above in Example 1 (speaking to Angelo and lifting his arms slightly before picking him up) for about 2 weeks. After 2 weeks, Angelo stopped being startled. After about 3 months, they noticed that if they

Recording Sheet 3-C

Child's name __Joey__ Observer's name __Dad__

Effectiveness of New Cues

Record your child's responses each time you try a new cue.

Date	Cue tried	Results
9/10/00	Put his hand in the bath water	He moved his hand.
9/12/00	Tried to get him to squeeze the sponge	He needed help.
9/14/00	Let him smell the shampoo	He became very quiet and alert.
9/14/00	Tapped him under the elbows	He put his arms up.

waited about 10 seconds before picking him up out of his wheelchair, he would lift up his arms indicating a desire to be picked up. Mrs. L was pleasantly surprised and said it reminded her of how her firstborn child, Andre, had held out his arms to be picked up when he was a baby.

After using the strategies described in Module 3, encourage the caregiver to record the child's behaviors by completing the module summary of accomplishments (see Appendixes D and E). This information may be shared with other caregivers or service providers.

Module 4

Establishing Turn Taking

RATIONALE

In children who develop typically, one of the earliest communication routines is infant–caregiver turn taking. The caregiver responds to the child's nonverbal signals to develop *contingency games*. These early games ensure that the caregiver and the child are *engaged* with one another and that this engagement can be extended across several turns. This turn taking eventually evolves into games, such as Peekaboo and Pat-a-cake, and serves as an important foundation for the development of conversations. For the child who has severe and multiple disabilities, however, the establishment of turn-taking routines may be very slow to develop. The focus of the curriculum now shifts from the caregiver to the child.

Once the child can request more of something as in the first objective of Module 4, caregivers expand the child's request for more into a series of turns. The caregivers' contingent responses to the child's behaviors will in turn motivate the child to understand cause and effect and to participate in social interactions.

GOAL

The child will participate in familiar turn-taking routines in which he or she can interact easily with the caregivers.

DIRECTIONS TO THE SERVICE PROVIDER

1. Read Module 4 and become familiar with the main ideas.
2. Review each objective before you plan to introduce it to the caregiver. Practice how you will explain key concepts and how you will demonstrate how to complete relevant forms.
3. Duplicate handouts for Module 4 to give to the caregiver when you introduce each objective.
4. Introduce Module 4 to the caregiver by providing the overview handout (see below and also Appendixes D and E).

	Overview of Module 4: Establishing Turn Taking
Rationale	For children who do not have disabilities, one of the earliest communication routines is what is called "turn taking." Not long after a child is born, he or she begins to engage in interactions with the primary caregiver in which each partner takes a turn. For example, a mother blows on her child's tummy, then the child gurgles, kicks, and then stops. The mother blows again, and the child takes another turn, then stops and waits again. Such turn taking ensures that the caregiver and the child are engaged or connected to one another communicatively and emotionally. Such turn taking eventually evolves into games like Peekaboo and Pat-a-cake. However, for the child who has disabilities, turn taking may be very slow to develop. Module 4 will show you some ways to encourage turn-taking routines and games with your child.
Goal	The goal of Module 4 is to develop and extend turn-taking routines with your child.
Activities	The first procedure in Module 4 will be to encourage your child to request more of something by interrupting a pleasurable activity. You will identify any existing turn-taking routines that you already do with your child and try to make them last longer by extending them across more turns. You will also learn to create new turn-taking routines in two ways. The first way begins with interrupting a pleasurable activity then extending the request for more over several turns. The second way of creating a new turn-taking activity is an imitation procedure in which you attempt to enter into an activity that the child is already doing by imitating his or her actions. These methods will encourage your child to participate in new turn-taking games.

OBJECTIVES AND PROCEDURES

After providing an overview of Module 4, introduce each objective. Each objective is listed here, followed by steps and examples. Blank forms for each example recording sheet are in Appendixes D and E.

Objective 4A

Teaching the Request for More

Using information gained in previous modules, caregivers will learn how to encourage children to request "more" of a desired food, object, or activity.

Step 1

With the caregiver, review the information about the child's preferences and dislikes that was recorded on Recording Sheet 2-A: Your Child's Preferences. Select a very high preference activity or food. Note changes in the child's likes and dislikes since Module 2. Some examples might include holding and rocking the child, brushing the child's hair with a soft brush, or playing some favorite music.

Step 2

Using information that the caregiver has previously provided on Recording Sheet 1-A: Typical Daily Activities, determine with the caregiver the most convenient opportunities throughout the day to make this preference available to the child. Two examples might be after lunch while Mom is watching television or after bath time.

Step 3

Begin the activity. After several seconds, interrupt the activity. Wait quietly for at least 15 seconds. Silently count to 15. If the child responds in a way that seems to indicate a desire for more of the activity, say, "Okay, you want more ____," and resume the activity. Practice this "interrupted routine" procedure with the caregiver several times.
Complete at least one trial and record it on Recording Sheet 4-A: Request for More: Interruption Plans. Ask the caregiver to try the interruption strategy over the next week.

Step 4

Caregivers can record the child's response to each interruption on Recording Sheet 4-A: Request for More: Interruption Plans that you began in Step 3. Or, if they prefer, they can simply summarize their experiences with this procedure at the end of the day or week.

Example 1

Josie loves to have her back massaged. Josie's mother rubs her back as usual, just before bedtime. Mother stops rubbing her back and waits quietly, doing nothing. After about 15

Recording Sheet 4-A

Child's name __Maria__   Observer's name __Mom__

Request for More: Interruption Plans

Describe the plan for interrupting your child's favorite activities, then record the results each time you use this plan.

Plan		Results		
Favorite activity	How will you interrupt this activity?	Date tried	How did your child respond?	Comments
Massage after bath	Stop rubbing her tummy	10/20/00	Maria made a sound.	
		11/13/00	She wiggled.	
Bouncing on Jolly Jumper	Stop bouncing her	10/26/00	She patted the ball.	
		11/20/00	She wiggled.	

seconds, Josie turns her head toward her mother and vocalizes. Her mother immediately begins to massage her back again, saying, "Oh, you want Mom to rub your back some more." She repeats this pattern two or three times. She notices that each time (after she interrupts the back rubbing), Josie turns her head a little more quickly.

Example 2

Mrs. F knows that rocking is one of Claudia's favorite activities. Although Mrs. F is very busy with her other children before and after school, she does enjoy watching television each afternoon from 2 to 3 P.M. During this time she sits in the rocking chair with Claudia and rocks back and forth. During a commercial, she stops rocking. Mrs. F watches Claudia carefully. After about 10 seconds, Claudia begins to squirm. She extends her back slightly and makes a fussing sound. Mrs. F says, "Oh, I guess you want to rock some more, don't you, Claudia?" and starts rocking again.

Note

 Often, the child's response may be very subtle (e.g., a slight change in body tension, a cessation of activity). It may take very careful observation to identify this response. In some cases, the child may produce several different responses but none consistently. For example, Claudia might fuss one time, squirm another, turn her head another time, and sometimes do nothing. In this situation, the caregiver may want to select only one of these (e.g., the one that occurs the most frequently or the one that is the easiest to recognize as a discrete behavior) to use as the request for more. In other cases, the child may produce a behavior that is harmful (e.g., bite his or her hand or slap his or her head). It is important not to reinforce these harmful behaviors but to instead identify a more acceptable behavior that can be shaped into a signal. This requires a great deal of self-discipline on the part of the caregiver. He or she must watch carefully and only resume the activity when the child produces that specific behavior and must ignore the other behaviors.

Step 5

Assist the caregiver in trying to extend the request for more response into a turn-taking game by interrupting and waiting several times. Try to extend the child's request for more across several turns so that it becomes a game.

Example 3

Mr. P stops pushing the swing and waits expectantly. Julie kicks. Mr. P pushes the swing three times and stops. Julie kicks. Mr. P pushes the swing a few times again and stops. Julie kicks. Mr. P starts to push again, saying, "OK. More swing!"

Example 4

Ms. H places her infant, Daniel, on her lap. Daniel has a moderate hearing loss and very low vision. Ms. H covers her face with a bright yellow washcloth. When Daniel squirms and vocalizes, she dramatically pulls the cloth away, saying, "Peek-a-boo!" When she says, "Peek-a-boo," she leans toward his cheek so he can feel the puff of air when she says, "Peek." She leans back, covers her face again, and waits. Daniel quickly responds again. Mother and Daniel are able to continue the game across six turns. At this point Daniel yawns, and Ms. H says, "OK, it's time for your nap, isn't it?"

Objective 4B

Developing Turn-Taking Games

Caregivers will identify and extend any current turn-taking routines and create new turn-taking games through imitation.

Step 1

Explain to caregivers what is meant by *turn-taking routines:* a type of social interaction that is characterized by mutual participation and engagement between the caregiver and the child in which the two participants take several turns contingent upon one another's behavior.

Example 1

Mother's turn:	She gently tickles the infant under chin; the infant laughs. The mother stops and waits.
Infant's turn:	Kicks his or her legs.
Mother's turn:	Tickles her infant again; the infant laughs. She waits.
Infant's turn:	Kicks his or her legs and vocalizes.
Mother's turn:	Tickles infant again; the infant smiles. The mother waits.
Infant's turn:	Kicks legs, waves his or her arms.

If possible, the service provider should use videotapes to demonstrate examples of such turn-taking routines. If the child does not currently engage in any turn taking, go on to the third step.

Step 2

Ask caregivers to try to identify any existing turn-taking interactions and to attempt to extend these for more turns. For example, if they currently play a very brief game of blowing on the child's tummy while diapering him or her, ask them to try to extend this game to six turns.

Step 3

Create new turn-taking games by imitating the child's behavior. When the child produces a behavior (e.g., makes a sound, pats the caregiver's hand, shakes a rattle), the caregiver can briefly produce that same behavior by imitating the child's action.

Step 4

Stop and wait for the child to resume the behavior.

Step 5

Imitate the child's behavior again, then stop and wait.

Step 6

Once the sequence is well established, the caregiver can try modifying the response. For example, if the child has been making the sound "uh uh uh" try presenting the sound "ee ee ee." Often, this will create a novel event, or *discrepancy* effect that is interesting to the child and can lead then to the child imitating the caregiver, rather than the other way around. It can also help prevent boredom and provide motivation for both the child and the caregiver to continue the game. Use Recording Sheet 4-B: Developing Turn-Taking Games (see Appendixes D and E) with the caregiver to list the child's preferred activities and how they may be developed into turn-taking games.

Example 2

Josie is patting her mother's arm with one hand. Her mother imitates this behavior for several turns by patting Josie's arm. Then her mother changes her response by patting Josie on both arms with two hands. Josie hesitates, recognizing that something is different. She then moves her other hand up and down while patting her mother's arm.

Objective 4C

Generalizing Turn-Taking Games

The caregiver will generalize the turn-taking games across people and environments.

Step 1

Caregivers can begin by playing previously established turn-taking games in a variety of situations and at different times of the day.

Example 1

Mother and Daniel always play the Peekaboo game just before nap time each day. Once the game is well established and can be extended across several turns, she begins to try to initiate the game when she is getting Daniel dressed in the morning. At first, Daniel doesn't respond to the game in this setting, but after a few tries he seems to remember the game.

Recording Sheet 4-B

Child's name __Maria__   Observer's name __Mom__

Developing Turn-Taking Games

Describe the plan for each game, then record the results each time you play the game with your child.

Plan		Results	
Favorite activity	What you will do?	Date tried	How did your child respond?
Bouncing on Jolly Jumper	Bounce her, stop and wait, then repeat each step	10/20/00	Maria laughed and rocked back and forth.
		10/23/00	She bounced and rocked back and forth.
Patting the highchair tray	Imitate Maria's patting the tray	10/26/00	She patted the tray, then stopped and did it again.
		10/28/00	She patted the tray, then stopped.

Step 2

Caregivers should encourage other people to play turn-taking games, especially other family members, teachers, and therapists. They can help these individuals recognize the specific communicative behaviors of the child. Use Recording Sheet 4-C: Generalizing Turn-Taking Games (see Appendixes D and E) to help the caregiver identify familiar turn-taking games that will be tried with new people or in different situations. Ask the caregiver to note the dates tried and the child's responses.

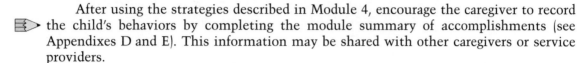
After using the strategies described in Module 4, encourage the caregiver to record the child's behaviors by completing the module summary of accomplishments (see Appendixes D and E). This information may be shared with other caregivers or service providers.

Recording Sheet 4-C

Child's name Mark

Observer's name Mom

Generalizing Turn-Taking Games

Describe the plan for each game, then record the results each time you play the game with your child.

Plan			Results
Turn-taking game	New person or place	Date tried	How did your child respond?
Patting the tray	With the babysitter at Mark's child care center	10/20/99	He looked at the babysitter's hand, then patted the tray.

Module 5

Encouraging Communicative Initiations

RATIONALE

A critical prerequisite for the development of communication is the child's discovery that he or she can initiate an interaction and have an effect on the world around him or her. The most powerful motivators for the development of communication are opportunities to obtain a desired object or activity, to reject a disliked object or activity, or to gain attention and interaction from a caregiver.

GOAL

The child will increase his or her rate of communicative initiation for the purposes of obtaining attention from significant caregivers, obtaining a desired object or pleasurable activity, and expressing rejection. The goal is to increase the child's control and initiation of those behaviors identified in earlier modules.

DIRECTIONS TO THE SERVICE PROVIDER

1. Read Module 5 and become familiar with the main ideas.
2. Review each objective before you plan to introduce it to the caregiver. Practice how you will explain key concepts and how you will demonstrate how to complete relevant forms.
3. Duplicate handouts for Module 5 to give to the caregiver when you introduce each objective.
4. Introduce Module 5 to the caregiver by providing the overview handout (see also Appendixes D and E).

	Overview of Module 5: Encouraging Communicative Initiations
Rationale	The most important goal of this curriculum is for your child to begin to use or to increase the use of communicative initiations. An important prerequisite to the development of communication is your child's discovery that he or she can have an effect on the environment through his or her own voluntary actions. As you learned in Modules 1, 2, and 4, the most powerful motivations for children with disabilities to communicate are opportunities to obtain a desired object or activity, to obtain a caregiver's attention, or to reject something they dislike.
Goal	The main goal of Module 5 is to increase your child's use of communicative behaviors to initiate interactions in order to get attention, to obtain a desired object or activity, or to reject something.
Activities	You will learn to use several specific strategies in order to increase your child's communications. You will learn to allow your child to reject something he or she doesn't want or is tired of. Another strategy you will learn is how to teach your child to initiate by delaying anticipated events in the daily routine. For example, you can get your child ready for his or her breakfast, but delay it a minute or two. Finally, you will learn some ways to encourage your child to communicate in order to get your attention by setting up an anticipated event but moving away from your child so he or she has to get your attention in order to start the desired activity.

OBJECTIVES AND PROCEDURES

After providing an overview of Module 5 (see above), introduce each objective. Each objective is listed here, followed by steps and examples. Blank forms for each example recording sheet are in Appendixes D and E.

Objective 5A

Initiating Rejection

Caregivers will learn to increase the child's initiations by responding to the child's expressions of rejection and encouraging the child to express rejection of a disliked food, object, or activity in selected situations.

Often one of the best ways to encourage the child with significant disabilities to communicate is to provide the opportunity to reject something that he or she dislikes.

Step 1

Using information obtained in Module 2 on Recording Sheet 2-A: Your Child's Preferences, assist caregivers in identifying objects and activities or situations that the child strongly dislikes.

Step 2

Suggest that caregivers try this procedure just a few times during a 2-week time period. Do not misuse this procedure! It should be used carefully, ensuring that the child does not become frustrated or angry. (See following Note on page 65.)

Step 3

The caregiver presents the disliked food, object, or activity to the child. As soon as the child produces a negative behavior, such as turning away, grimacing, or swiping at the object, say, "Okay. I guess you don't like the _____. No more _____." Recording Sheet 5-A: Rejecting a Disliked Object or Activity (see Appendixes D and E) may be used with the caregiver to identify the disliked activity, to plan how to respond, and to record results.

Example 1

Jay's mother places Jay prone (on his stomach) on a blanket on the floor. Although he is usually comfortable in this position for a few minutes, he eventually grows tired of it and starts to cry. Using the above procedure, Jay's mother will be alert to Jay's first sign of protest, which is a fussing sound. When she hears this fussing, before he begins to cry, she says, "Oh, I guess you want to turn over now, huh?" and turns him over onto his back.

Example 2

Monica enjoys soft classical music, but she is often (but not always) annoyed by loud rock music. Monica's brother turns on his favorite rock music and turns up the volume a bit. Monica extends her arms and turns her head away. Her brother immediately turns off the music saying, "Okay, I guess you're not in the mood today for rock music."

Example 3

Carmen is in her highchair at the family dinner table. Her dad is feeding her her favorite baby food, mashed sweet potato. The family is having cooked carrots, which Carmen hates. Carmen's dad mashes a bit of carrot and brings it to Carmen's mouth. Carmen smells the carrot and immediately brings her hand up to her mouth and begins to fuss. Dad says, "Okay, no carrot. Here's more sweet potato."

Recording Sheet 5-A

Child's name ___Maya___   Observer's name ___Grandma___

Rejecting a Disliked Object or Activity

Disliked activity	How do you expect your child to communicate dislike?	How will you respond?	Date tried
Putting on glasses	Make noise and wiggle her head.	Give her a favorite cookie.	11/16/00
Washing her face	Squirm and whimper.	Sing to her.	11/20/00

Note

 If what the child dislikes is a necessary activity, it is not appropriate to use this procedure. For example, the child cannot reject a prescribed medicine or a necessary health procedure. Caregivers should, however, verbally acknowledge the child's discomfort, such as by saying, "I'm sorry. I know you hate this, but you have to take your medicine."

Objective 5B

Increasing Initiations

Caregivers will learn to increase the child's initiations by delaying an anticipated activity.

Note

 If the child's environment has been predictable, he or she will learn to anticipate certain activities and events. If the activity is one that the child finds pleasurable, a delay in this expected activity may encourage communicative initiation as the child attempts to request it. This communication is more difficult than the request for more because the child is not already engaged in the activity.

◆ Step 1

 Based on Recording Sheet 3-A: Predictable Daily Activities, ask caregivers to identify the predictable activity that is most pleasurable to the child. Or, use high-preference activities listed on Recording Sheet 4-A to teach the child the request for more or use turn-taking games established in Module 4.

◆ Step 2

Present all the normal cues and sequence of actions leading up to that activity. But do not actually start the activity.

◆ Step 3

Delay the onset of the expected activity for up to 2 or 3 minutes. The caregiver waits expectantly. He or she should observe the child carefully.

Note

 Time is critical here. Often, children with severe and multiple disabilities become passive simply because they are not given enough time to respond!

Step 4

If the child demonstrates any behavior that the caregiver interprets as a request for the activity, the caregiver should acknowledge that it is time for that activity and begin as usual.

Example 1

Joshua always gets excited when it's time for his bath. His mother engages in the usual sequence of events that typically lead up to bath time: She carries Joshua into the bathroom, turns on the water in the tub, takes off his clothes, pours bubble bath into the tub, and lets Joshua feel the bubbles with his hand and foot. Normally, at this point Joshua's mother would say, "Okay, in the tub you go" while placing him in the tub. However, using the delay procedure described above, she waits quietly and does not put him in the tub. After about 1 minute, Joshua begins to bounce on her lap and vocalize. Mother immediately says, "Okay, in the tub you go" and places him in the tub.

This example may be used to demonstrate to the caregiver how to record a trial of the delay procedure on a blank Recording Sheet 5-B: Increasing Initiation (see Appendixes D and E).

Step 5

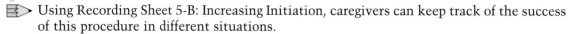 Using Recording Sheet 5-B: Increasing Initiation, caregivers can keep track of the success of this procedure in different situations.

Note

 A child who has developed object permanence and an understanding that objects exist even when they are not present (mental representation) can then learn to initiate requests for objects or activities that are not immediately present and for which there are no cues.

Example 2

Matthew's mom sits down with Matthew and puts him on her knee. She turns on his favorite tape of the Barney song. This is the usual set up for bouncing him on her knee—a game Matthew loves. However, she does not move. Instead, she simply waits. Matthew does not move. He is very still—as though he is trying to figure out what is wrong. After about 30 seconds, Mom moves her knee just slightly. Matthew responds with his usual head bob, and the game proceeds as usual. Later in the day, Mom sets up the situation again. She places Matthew on her knee, turns on the tape, and waits. This time after about 15 seconds, Matthew bobs his head, and Mom immediately starts bouncing him on her knee. Matthew smiles. He has discovered *he* can control the game!

Recording Sheet 5-B

Child's name __Carmen__   Observer's name __Dad__

Increasing Initiation

First describe the plan, then record each time you try it.

Plan			Results	
Preferred activity	Usual sequence of cues	Where or how will you delay?	Date tried	How did your child respond?
Being fed, something she likes	I tap her lips and chin with the spoon first.	I will let her smell it first and wait to feed her.	9/4/00	She taps her lips and her fingers.
			9/5/00	She flaps her hands and feet.

Objective 5C

Intentional Attention Getting

The caregiver will learn how to encourage the child to initiate intentionally to obtain the caregiver's attention.

Note

 A critical behavior in the development of communication skills is the child's desire and ability to obtain the caregiver's attention, either for the purpose of using the caregiver as a tool to get a desired object or activity or simply to obtain the caregiver's social interaction. It is also critical that the child learns to engage in what is called distal communication. *That is, the child must realize that he or she can use communication even when the caregiver is not in close proximity. This is a difficult behavior to teach, especially when a child's distal senses of vision or hearing are impaired. For some young children with severe or multiple sensory disabilities, this goal of distal communication may never be fully realized. Nevertheless, caregivers should continue to encourage this behavior. This objective builds upon the previous objectives in an attempt to encourage true (noncued) intentional initiation. If the child is already using behaviors to get attention, skip this objective. Simply list these behaviors and describe their purposes.*

Step 1

After the child consistently requests more of an interrupted activity, set up the activity as usual but delay the start of the activity, as in the previous objective (e.g., place the infant in his or her highchair, but do not put anything on the tray).

Step 2

Instead of waiting expectantly and maintaining close proximity to the infant as in the previous objective, the caregiver should engage in some other activity (e.g., reading the newspaper, washing the dishes, cooking) somewhat removed from the child (e.g., across the room). However, he or she must be close enough to be able to hear and see the child's response.

Step 3

See if the child will initiate to try to get the caregiver's attention to begin the activity. If the child demonstrates a signal behavior (e.g., vocalizes, bangs the tray, waves his or her arms), the caregiver immediately approaches the child saying something like, "Oops, I forgot you were ready for your cereal. Here it is."

Example 1

At bath time José's mother takes José into the bathroom and runs the water into the tub. She places José in his adaptive seat near the tub but does not take his clothes off. Instead, she starts cleaning some shelves in the bathroom. She does not talk to José. José starts to squirm and fuss. His mother immediately approaches him, saying, "Okay. You're right, it's time for your bath."

Example 2

Susanna's mother has been using the interruption strategy during rocking to get Susanna to request more. Susanna will fairly consistently kick her legs to get her mom to start rocking again. Today Susanna's mother sits down in the rocking chair and puts Susanna on a blanket on the floor near the chair, rather than holding her in her lap. Instead of rocking, she starts reading the paper. After about 3 minutes, Susanna starts kicking and vocalizing. Susanna's mother immediately puts her paper down and says, "Oh, okay Susanna! You want to rock," and she picks her up and begins rocking. This is really the first time Susanna has initiated an interaction with her mother.

Step 4

The caregiver should also be very alert to the child's attempts to simply get the caregiver to pay attention to him or her by vocalizing or picking him or her up. In other words, the child is not using the caregiver as a means to an end to get something else but simply wants the caregiver to be close or wants to be able to hear the caregiver's voice.

Example 3

When Noriko wakes up from her nap, she begins to fuss. Her mother responds quickly by going to her room and picking her up, saying, "You woke up from your nap. It's time to get up and have your bottle!"

Example 4

Carrie is in her playpen in the living room. Her big sister, Mary, is in the kitchen starting dinner. She hears Carrie vocalizing, as though she is hollering to get Mary's attention. Mary calls to her from the kitchen, "I'll be there in a minute. Sister's in the kitchen now." She then goes into the living room and picks Carrie up, saying, "Here I am. Were you missing me?"

Example 5

Jackie's parents both noticed that when they were engaged in conversation with each other, across the room from Jackie, she would eventually begin to cry. They actually commented that they found this irritating and that they really didn't seem to have much time to talk to each other anymore. After observing this scenario very carefully in Module 1, they learned that before Jackie actually began to cry, she would often make quieter sounds and move her head from side to side. They decided to try to notice and respond to her vocal behavior before it evolved into a full blown cry. They would begin talking with each other. Then, as soon as Jackie vocalized, one of them would go to her, pick her up and say, "Okay, you want to join our conversation too, huh?" They found that they could resume their conversation while holding Jackie and that she was quiet and content.

Recording Sheet 5-C

Child's name __Terisa__   Observer's name __Aunt Doris__

Initiating Attention

First describe the plan, then record each time you try it.

Plan		Results	
What activity will you delay and how will you delay it?	What will you do while delaying the start?	Date tried	How did your child respond?
In the middle of feeding her, I stop for 5 minutes.	I will wait to see what happens.	11/10/00	She picks up her arms and starts kicking.
		11/13/00	She bangs her hands on the high chair.

Note

Some caregivers may report that their children already attempt to gain their attention too often. Thus, they may not wish to pursue this objective. The service provider may attempt to clarify whether it is actually the frequency of initiation or the way in which the child initiates that the caregiver finds unacceptable. Also, some caregivers may believe that responding immediately to a young child's demand for attention— especially to the child's fussing—may result in spoiling the child. However, the service provider can explain that an immediate response is necessary in order for the child with severe and multiple disabilities to learn the important skill of initiating communication.

Step 5

 Using Recording Sheet 5-C: Initiating Attention (see Appendixes D and E), the caregivers can record the child's behavior each time they try this procedure. Or, if they prefer, caregivers may wish to simply summarize at the end of the day or week how the child responded to the situation and whether they have seen any increase in the child's attempts to gain attention.

 After using the strategies described in Module 5, encourage the caregiver to record the child's behaviors by completing the module summary of accomplishments (see Appendixes D and E). This information may be shared with other caregivers or service providers.

Final Note

The ultimate goal of this first stage of development of early communication is for the child with multiple and severe disabilities to be able to initiate an interaction and eventually to initiate a request for a particular thing. Although this may be a relatively easy achievement for most infants and young children, it offers a great challenge for children with severe multiple disabilities. The child who learns to initiate to obtain interaction or who learns to use the caregiver to obtain desired objects or activities has achieved a significant milestone. After attaining the skills identified in Modules 4 and 5, a child should be ready to benefit from naturalistic strategies that support the continued development of communication skills.

After completing all five modules, caregivers will have developed important skills that can continue to be used to support the child's learning and development. At this point, service providers can now take advantage of the many special education curricula and guidelines available to assist children with disabilities in the development of intentional communication and to teach caregivers to use specific kinds of communicative interaction strategies to facilitate the young child's learning of language or other symbolic communication systems.

References

Brazelton, T.B. (1984). Neonatal assessment scale. *Clinics in Developmental Medicine, 88.* London: Spastics International Medical Publisher.

Chen, D. (1996). Parent–infant communication: Early intervention for very young children with visual impairment or hearing loss. *Infants and Young Children, 9*(1), 1–12.

Chen, D., Friedman, C.T., & Calvello, G. (1990). *Parents and visually impaired infants: Parent observation protocol.* Louisville, KY: American Printing House for the Blind.

Chen, D., Klein, M.D., & Haney, M. (2000). *Promoting learning through active interactions: An instructional video.* Baltimore: Paul H. Brookes Publishing Co.

Guess, D., Seigel-Causey, E., Roberts, S., Guy, B., & Rues, J. (1993). Analysis of state organizational patterns among students with profound disabilities. *Journal of The Association for Persons with Severe Handicaps, 18,* 93–108.

McCollum, J.A., & McBride, S.L. (1997). Ratings of parent–infant interactions: Raising questions of cultural validity. *Topics in Early Childhood Special Education, 17*(4), 494–519.

Sameroff, A.J., & Chandler, M.J. (1975). Reproductive risk and the continuum of caretaking causality. In F.D. Horowitz (Ed.), *Review of child development research* (Vol. 4, pp. 187–244). Chicago: University of Chicago Press.

Vygotsky, L.S. (1978). *Mind and society.* Cambridge, MA: Harvard University Press.

Appendix A

Using Videotaped Observations

Videotaping is a powerful tool for assisting caregivers and service providers to observe carefully a child's behaviors, particularly those that are subtle, fleeting, and multidimensional. Many children with severe and multiple disabilities demonstrate muted, inconsistent, and puzzling nonverbal behaviors that are difficult to interpret. Systematic observations of the child in a variety of activities enable the caregiver and the service provider to hypothesize about and then to identify the communicative meaning of selected child behaviors. Caregivers have indicated that videotaping enables them not only to observe their child's behaviors but also to reflect on their own interactions (Chen, Friedman, & Calvello, 1990).

In the *PLAI* model, the service provider and the caregiver view video segments of selected activities with the child for three reasons: 1) to discuss the meaning of the child's behaviors; 2) to identify enjoyable aspects of the interaction; and 3) to discuss ways that the interaction might be adapted to support the child's understanding of the activity. In this way, caregivers develop their own observation skills, are better able to interpret their child's communicative behaviors, and recognize strategies that elicited and supported interaction with their child. Although being videotaped is not a natural or comfortable process, in field-test activities the majority of caregivers who viewed videotapes of themselves and their children found the experience to be very helpful. Some caregivers reported that they did not like being videotaped and felt as if they "rushed" to complete the activity while being taped. Two caregivers indicated that when they were being videotaped they were reluctant to sing to their children. One family did not want to view the tapes because of the severity of their child's medical needs and disabilities. Yet, some caregivers recommended that the videotape process be used more frequently and felt that being videotaped gave them a chance to "show off." Many families view the videotapes as an audiovisual baby book and plan to duplicate copies for relatives.

Before making any arrangements, offer caregivers the option of whether they want to use the videotape strategy. Respect the caregivers' wishes if they do not want to be videotaped. Initially, caregivers may be nervous about being videotaped or may feel threatened by the prospect. It may be difficult for some caregivers to look at a video of themselves and their children. Other caregivers will become more comfortable with the idea as they build a relationship with you.

MAKING VIDEOTAPED OBSERVATIONS

There are several tips that service providers can use in order to make the use of videotaping easier and more productive.

Obtaining Equipment

1. Be familiar with your program's policy regarding the use of equipment and insurance coverage.
2. Obtain a camcorder, read the manual, and become familiar with the parts and features of the camcorder. Practice using the camcorder, learn how to hold and focus it, try out different shots, and insert the date code. Review your practice tape so that you can improve your camerawork.
3. Become familiar with the proper handling, packing procedures, and troubleshooting tips noted in the manual. Handle the camcorder carefully. Do not point the camcorder directly into a strong light source such as the sun, and do not store it in the car. Keep it dry, dust-free, and safe from extreme temperatures.
4. In preparing to make a videotape, make sure that the battery pack is fully charged and a blank tape is available.

Planning Steps

1. Identify how and when videotaping will be used to implement the *PLAI* curriculum.
2. Discuss the purpose and procedures involved in the videotaping strategy (i.e., "to help us recognize how your child communicates and figure out ways to expand on this communication").
3. According to the policy of your program, obtain signed consent from the caregivers with a clear written agreement of how the videotape will be used and ensure confidentiality.
4. Look at the area in which you will be making the videotape. Ask for permission to remove toys or other obstacles that may be hazardous when you are walking with the camcorder.
5. Eliminate background noises (e.g., ask the caregiver to turn off the radio or television), explaining that the microphone in the camcorder will pick up all sounds.
6. Depending on the type of camcorder, adjust lighting accordingly. Rooms with dark wood panels tend to look darker on the videotape, and an extra light source may be needed. Do not shoot scenes with people in front of a window or other bright light

source because the backlight will cause a "hot" or very bright element in the picture, and other parts of the picture will appear washed out.

Making the Videotape

1. With the caregiver, identify the activity to be videotaped. Use Recording Sheet 1-A: Typical Daily Activities to select an activity.
2. Determine how much and which parts of the activity will be videotaped. The observation will not be useful if the videotape is too long. About 10 minutes of taping is needed to provide enough time to observe and discuss selected aspects of the activity.
3. Let the caregiver know that the taping can be stopped for interruptions and other needs (e.g., telephone calls, child gets fussy). Discuss in advance whether you will stop taping for certain interruptions.
4. Encourage the caregiver to be as natural as possible and do what he or she usually does.
5. Videotape the selected activity.
6. Change the shot size (e.g., wide shot, bust shot, close up, zoom in) slowly and progressively only if necessary to capture what you want to observe. Hold the camcorder steady or use a tripod.
7. Label the tape, and remove the tab to protect the recording.
8. Thank the caregiver for participating in the videotaping process.

Previewing the Tape

1. Preview the tape before the next home visit with the caregiver.
2. Select the segment for review, and use it to discuss the relevant objective:
   - Note the child's behaviors and responses to the caregiver's interactions.
   - Identify how the caregiver communicates with the child.
   - List questions to ask the caregiver and practice asking them, such as "Why do you think Mary moves her hand when you massage her legs?"
   - Develop suggestions for increasing communication with the child, related to specific *PLAI* objectives.

Implementing Modules on Videotape

Videotaped segments are helpful for implementing the first four modules of the curriculum. Here are some ideas for using videotape for some objectives.

The goal of Module 1 is to assist caregivers in understanding their child's cues by developing a detailed picture of the ways in which the child expresses attention and interest, internal states such as pleasure and discomfort, and needs and desires. For the second objective in Module 1, caregivers will watch a videotape of the child in an activity, for example, mealtime. In viewing the videotape with the caregiver, discuss the child's state of arousal while he or she is being placed in the highchair, fed, and cleaned up. For the third objective of Module 1, caregivers should watch videotape of the child playing alone or with the caregiver. In viewing the videotape with the caregiver, identify a specific child behavior, (e.g., crying, smiling, moving a foot) and then look at what happens just before and right after the behavior. This way, a caregiver may be engaged in a discussion about antecedents and consequences and develop an understanding of behavior analysis.

The goal of Module 2 is to assist caregivers in identifying what their child enjoys and what he or she dislikes. For the second objective of Module 2, you should videotape the child playing alone or in daily activities with others. In viewing the tape with the caregiver, identify how the child responds to different toys, people, or activities. This way some of the child's preferences and dislikes may be determined.

The goal of Module 3 is to assist caregivers in establishing predictable routines that will enable the child to anticipate activities through recognition of specific cues. For the third objective of Module 3, videotape the child and the caregiver in a daily activity (e.g., eating a meal, playing, dressing). In viewing the tape with the caregiver, discuss when cues may be added and the kinds of cues that might help their child to anticipate the steps in the activity.

The goal of Module 4 is to assist caregivers in developing a repertoire of familiar turn-taking routines in which the child can participate easily. For the first objective of Module 4, you can videotape the child and the caregiver in a favorite activity (e.g., eating, swinging, movement games). View the videotape with the caregiver, and discuss when the caregiver might pause to encourage the child to request more through nonverbal behavior. For the second objective, videotape the child and caregiver in a familiar turn-taking game (e.g., Peek-a-boo). View the tape with the caregiver, and discuss how the game might be expanded or changed.

REVIEWING THE VIDEOTAPE WITH THE CAREGIVER

First, provide review and feedback on the videotape that is respectful and sensitive to an individual caregiver's concerns and feelings. The purpose of the review is to support the caregiver's reflection on his or her interaction skills and observation of the child's behaviors. Be aware of the caregiver's reaction to viewing the videotape.

Second, view the tape with the caregiver and emphasize the caregiver's skill and effectiveness in communicating with the child and the child's specific responses to the caregivers (e.g., "She really settled down when you picked her up"; "He got so excited when he saw you"). Use the following review and feedback strategies as appropriate:

- Focus on what's happening on the tape.
- Emphasize what seems enjoyable (e.g., "Looks like you're both having a good time"; "You really know his cues"; "Just look at how much she loves the horsy game").
- Comment on the child's behavior or response to the caregiver (e.g., "He leaned toward you after you touched his arm"; "Oh boy, he's tired").
- Ask the caregiver how he or she knew how to respond to the child (e.g., "How did you know she wanted more of that?"; "How did you know that he was hungry?").
- Ask the caregiver about selected child behaviors (e.g., "Why does he keep tossing that toy out of the tub?"; "Why does she move her hand when you're putting on her diaper?").

- Discuss specific objectives with the caregiver (e.g., "Let's try to figure out where to use a touch cue during this activity"; "Are there other little games that he seems to like?").

These strategies focus on the strengths of both the caregiver and the child and assist the caregiver in developing keen observation skills. In this way, the caregiver receives positive feedback about his or her interactions with the child.

Using Videos to Document Change

Planned videotaping of the caregiver and child in a typical activity provides a valuable means of documenting the child's progress and the effectiveness of the *PLAI* curriculum. For evaluation purposes, the caregiver and the child should be videotaped in the same situation more than once (i.e., before beginning the *PLAI* curriculum, after Module 3, and after completing the curriculum). These tapes may be reviewed with caregivers to identify or to reflect on observed changes in the caregiver's responses to the child's behaviors, in use of cues, in types of games, and in the child's communication.

As discussed previously, the use of videotaping as an intervention strategy should be very individualized and dependent on the caregiver's choice. Each family is unique, and every caregiver is different. Some parents may feel saddened by viewing the child's very slow progress and severe disabilities. Other parents may find the videotaping process very satisfying as a documentation of changes in their child's development. Even when a child has made developmental progress, the early tapes may bring back emotions related to the child's medical needs in the early days. If a family elects to use videotaping as part of the *PLAI* curriculum, they should receive a copy of each segment or a complete tape upon completion of the modules.

Appendix B

Data Collection and Recording Sheets

Service providers should first complete the *Caregiver Interview* by discussing the questions with the caregiver. A blank copy is provided in Appendixes D and E. This process helps both the service provider and the caregiver to identify the child's communicative behaviors and to initiate a discussion of the *PLAI* curriculum. The *Caregiver Interview* should also be completed by the child's family and other caregivers (e.g., child care providers, teachers at center-based programs) as appropriate. This interview provides baseline data on the child's communicative behaviors that may be used in identifying changes in the child's communication.

USE OF RECORDING SHEETS

Each of the five modules in the curriculum has a set of recording sheets to support the implementation of specific strategies. Sample recording sheets can be found with the discussion of how to introduce and use each module. A blank copy of all recording sheets is contained in English in Appendix D and in Spanish in Appendix E for service providers to duplicate and use when implementing this curriculum. Information obtained on the recording sheets in early modules is used in later ones. Each objective has its own recording sheet.

DATA COLLECTION

This curriculum recognizes the importance of supporting child development within the natural environments of the child's family and daily life. The authors are also well aware

	Understanding Your Child's Cues	
Module 1	**Goal**	**Recording Sheets for Each Objective**
	Caregivers will have a detailed picture of the ways in which the child expresses attention and interest; internal states, such as pleasure and discomfort; and needs and desires.	1. Recording Sheet 1-A: Typical Daily Activities 2. Recording Sheet 1-B: Categories of States of Arousal 3. Recording Sheet 1-C: Observations of Your Child's Responses to Daily Activities. Use information from Recording Sheet 1-A to develop a more detailed understanding of the child's reactions. 4. Recording Sheet 1-D: Your Child's Strategies and Purposes for Getting Attention 5. Update information on the *Caregiver Interview*.

	Identifying Your Child's Preferences	
Module 2	**Goal**	**Recording Sheets for Each Objective**
	Caregivers will develop a thorough understanding of what the child enjoys and what he or she dislikes.	1. Recording Sheet 2-A: Your Child's Preferences Use information from Recording Sheet 1-A: Typical Daily Activities. 2. Recording Sheet 2-B: Your Child's Responses to People, Objects, and Activities

	Establishing Predictable Routines	
Module 3	**Goal**	**Recording Sheets for Each Objective**

	Caregivers will create a daily routine that includes several predictable events that the child can anticipate through recognition of certain cues such as sounds, sights, or other sensations.	1. Recording Sheet 3-A: Predictable Daily Activities
		   Use information from Recording Sheet 1-A: Typical Daily Activities.
		2. Recording Sheet 3-B: Subroutines and Cues
		   Use information gathered about the child's learning style and needs.
		3. Recording Sheet 3-C: Effectiveness of New Cues
		   Use information gathered about the child's learning style and needs. Refer to Recording Sheet 3-B: Subroutines and Cues.

	Establishing Turn Taking	
Module 4	**Goal**	**Recording Sheets for Each Objective**
	The child will participate in familiar turn-taking routines in which he or she can interact easily with caregivers.	1. Recording Sheet 4-A: Request for More: Interruption Plans Use information from Recording Sheet 2-A: Your Child's Preferences 2. Recording Sheet 4-B: Developing Turn-Taking Games 3. Recording Sheet 4-C: Generalizing Turn-Taking Games

	Encouraging Communicative Initiations	
Module 5	**Goal**	**Recording Sheets for Each Objective**

	The child will increase his or her rate of initiations for the purposes of obtaining a desired object or pleasurable event and expressing rejection.	1. Recording Sheet 5-A: Rejecting a Disliked Object or Activity
		   Use information from Recording Sheet 2-A: Your Child's Preferences.
		2. Recording Sheet 5-B: Increasing Initiation
		   Use information from Recording Sheet 3-A: Predictable Daily Activities, Recording Sheet 4-A: Request for More: Interruption Plans, or Recording Sheet 4-B: Developing Turn-Taking Games.
		3. Recording Sheet 5-C: Initiating Attention

of the potential intrusiveness of careful data recording when designing the curriculum. Nevertheless, there are several reasons for the inclusion of data recording procedures in this curriculum:

1. The behavioral cues of children with severe and multiple disabilities are often difficult to identify and to interpret. Careful observation and recording may be necessary in order to understand subtle, infrequent, and inconsistent behaviors.
2. In order for some of these children to learn, caregivers must learn to be extremely consistent in their routines and use of cues. It may be very difficult to maintain this consistency over time and across multiple caregivers without written documentation.
3. Change often occurs slowly with these children. Caregivers may become discouraged if they do not sense that the child is learning. Ongoing progress monitoring can provide concrete evidence of the child's development.
4. It is also important to know if a particular intervention is not working. Record keeping can provide valuable feedback indicating whether a procedure should be changed.
5. The need to record certain observations and activities can provide an organizational structure that motivates family members to implement the curriculum in a consistent way.

SUGGESTIONS FOR USING RECORDING SHEETS WITH CAREGIVERS

Despite its importance, data collection can be a difficult and tedious task. The skilled service provider will develop ways of tailoring record keeping for each family to prevent it from becoming overly burdensome. Some families—although not the majority—actually enjoy the data recording process and use of the recording sheets. Some caregivers seem to enjoy the concrete task of recording the child's behavior or recording their own activities. For these families, the service provider can demonstrate how the recording sheet is used and simply leave it with the caregiver to be completed by the next visit.

The recording sheet is very useful for structuring conversations with caregivers about strategies introduced in each objective. The service provider should introduce the recording sheet to the caregiver and discuss its use. Next, he or she should demonstrate how to use the sheet by observing the child and making notes on the form. Then, he or she may ask the caregiver to note his or her observations as they both observe the child. Finally, the service provider might ask the caregiver to try using the form during the next few days. In this way, the caregiver may become more comfortable in using the recording sheets. Blank copies of recording sheets are provided in English in Appendix D and in Spanish in Appendix E.

Some families find the process of data recording to be very difficult. In these cases, the service provider may need to do some of the data recording. Although obviously for some objectives this is not practical, there will be certain observations or activities that the service provider can do with the caregiver during a regular visit. The appropriate entries can be jotted down on the recording sheet at that time. This can then be compared with a similar observation during the following visit. Between visits, caregivers can be encouraged to try to carry out similar activities and to make whatever notations they are comfortable with.

A variation on this procedure would be for the service provider to make a telephone call a few days after a visit and ask whether family members had been able to use the activity or make the observations suggested in the module. The service provider then fills out the recording sheet, based on the caregiver's report.

Finally, some families will be willing and able to use recording sheets but may have difficulty in their busy schedules remembering or finding time to complete it. Here again, a reminder telephone call can be helpful. Prior to the next visit, the service provider can call caregivers to remind them to use the activities and strategies and to complete the recording sheet to whatever extent they can.

Appendix C

Background, Development, and Field-Test of the Curriculum

BACKGROUND OF THE CURRICULUM

Project PLAI: Promoting Learning through Active Interaction was a 4-year (9/1/94–2/28/99) research-to-practice project funded by the U.S. Department of Education to develop and validate an early communication curriculum for infants whose multiple disabilities include visual impairment and hearing loss. The project represented a significant collaboration between California State University–Northridge, the SKI*HI Institute, Utah State University, and public and private agencies serving infants and young children with multiple disabilities and their families.

In the first year of the project, the initial format and strategies of the curriculum were developed based on a thorough review of the literature and on observations of 11 young children (18–40 months of age) with multiple disabilities and their parents. From 1995 to 1998, the *PLAI* curriculum was field tested in southern California and then in Utah, by training service providers to use the curriculum with families. Initially, 34 infants and families (20 in southern California and 14 in Utah) began the curriculum. However, because of the children's medical needs, several families were unable to complete the process. A total of 25 infants and their caregivers completed all five modules of the curriculum. Many of these children had seizures, required medication, and needed other medical treatments (e.g., hospitalization, gastrostomy tube, respirator, tracheotomy, oximeter, cardiorespiratory monitor). Although hearing aids and glasses were prescribed for some children, they were either not obtained or they were not worn consistently. The children's vision problems included cortical visual impairment, refractive errors, retinal problems, coloboma, microphthalmia, and congenital ocular anomalies.

Five infants were completely blind; most of the other infants demonstrated some functional vision use. Their hearing losses ranged from mild to profound. Those children with mild to moderate losses or central auditory disorders did not respond consistently to sound. All children demonstrated moderate to profound developmental delays. These young children ranged between the ages of 8 and 33 months (mean age of 19.8 months) when they began the curriculum, and they were between the ages of 14 and 50 months (mean age of 31.6 months) when they completed it.

The *PLAI* curriculum was implemented successfully by caregivers of diverse backgrounds, with appropriate support from their service providers. These 25 families represented diverse educational levels (from parents who had not completed elementary school to those with advanced graduate degrees), socioeconomic backgrounds, and cultural backgrounds (African American, Hispanic, and Euro-Americans). Eight families spoke Spanish.

Sixteen service providers from six different programs in southern California and Utah implemented the curriculum successfully with families. These providers had a variety of qualifications: One was a paraprofessional (high school graduate and parent of a child with a disability); several had a bachelor's degree in child development; and many had credentials or master's degrees in such areas as hearing impairments, visual impairments, deafblindness, severe disabilities, orientation and mobility, and early childhood special education.

Most service providers participating in the project in southern California were not familiar with the key concepts of the curriculum or with direct and systematic instruction. They required significant support in explaining the modules to caregivers. These difficulties resulted in the first three modules taking several months to complete. However, once service providers and families became familiar with the curriculum, then implementation became easier and the modules were completed more quickly. Families took between 6 and 21 months to complete the curriculum (an average of 13.8 months).

EVALUATION PROCEDURES

A significant amount of data, both qualitative and quantitative, were collected for each child, caregiver, and service provider. Data included initial interviews; videotaped observations from baseline and after Modules 1, 3, 4, and 5; recording sheets and feedback forms for each module; focus group input; and follow-up interviews.

Videotapes of play and bath time interactions were coded to identify both the adult's and the child's characteristics in the interaction, types of responses and initiations, and the types of cues used by the caregiver. Findings indicate that 24 of 25 caregivers benefited from the curriculum's emphasis on consistent and appropriate use of cues with their children and on turn-taking strategies to support early communication. On ratings of caregiver interaction, an increase in elaborativeness noted between baseline and post–Module 3 is fairly consistent with the increase in the use of cues. Elaborativeness involves complementing and extending the child's actions and responding to behaviors that may be interpreted as communicative. It includes adding cues to the interactive situation to facilitate the child's understanding. In the first three modules of the *PLAI* curriculum, emphasis is placed on observing and interpreting the child's behaviors as well as use of cues, thus an increase in these skills suggests success in meeting the goals of Modules 1–3. The increase in both directiveness and sensitivity between baseline and post–Module 5 also supports the curriculum as an effective instructional tool for supporting caregiver interactions and early communication with young children who have severe and multiple disabilities. Modules 4 and 5 emphasize attending to and responding to the child's subtle cues that may be interpreted as requests for more and turn-taking behaviors. Sensitivity reflects the caregivers' awareness of the child's signals and their quick and appropriate response to these, behaviors that are directly taught in the *PLAI* curriculum.

Directiveness includes prompting the child to get a response and directing a child in what to do until an appropriate response is attained. The emphasis on developing the child's turn-taking and initiating skills found in Modules 4 and 5 support an increase in caregivers' directive behaviors as the caregiver may need to be more directive initially in order to elicit a response from a child with severe and multiple disabilities (e.g., set up a specific activity, provide a clear pause, wait for the child's response, prompt a response if needed).

We conducted annual focus group meetings in California and Utah with caregivers and service providers to obtain feedback and evaluate the curriculum process. Caregivers' repeated use of key words and concepts emphasized by the curriculum indicates that they understood the objectives of the curriculum. Most caregivers could identify strategies they found particularly successful as well as ones they would continue to use with their child.

Service providers also seemed to benefit from their participation in *Project PLAI*. In particular, for service providers in California, the two features of the curriculum that seemed most useful were the project's emphasis on a collaborative process with caregivers and on specific strategies for developing communicative behaviors with these young children who have severe and multiple disabilities. In Utah, the service providers, who were generally more knowledgeable about working with families and about specific early communication strategies, also benefited from the systematic and individualized application of these strategies as emphasized in the *PLAI* curriculum. Service providers indicated that they had also successfully used the *PLAI* strategies with other students who had intensive communication needs, including elementary and high-school age children with severe and multiple disabilities. Overall, we can infer that project participants felt that they had learned helpful strategies from the *PLAI* curriculum. Information on the use of anticipatory cues was particularly meaningful, but service providers and caregivers also learned to be better observers of their children and better interpreters of the meaning of their children's behaviors. Participation in the project seemed to support an increase in communication between caregivers and children, resulting in the children's increased awareness of activities and people in the environment.

Appendix D

Handouts in English

Module 1: Understanding Your Child's Cues

Goal	Objectives
Caregivers will have a detailed picture of the ways in which the child expresses attention and interest; internal states such as pleasure and discomfort; and needs and desires.	1. Caregivers will describe the child's typical day. 2. Caregivers will learn to identify the child's different states. 3. Through careful observation of antecedent events and consequences, caregivers will develop a clear understanding of the child's typical reactions to routines and activities. 4. Caregivers will identify and describe ways in which the child obtains attention from the caregiver and for what purposes. 5. Caregivers will describe how the child reacts to and expresses external states and feelings.

Module 2: Identifying Your Child's Preferences

Goal	Objectives
Caregivers will develop a thorough understanding of what the child enjoys and what he or she dislikes.	1. Caregivers will generate a detailed list of people, objects, and activities that they believe the child enjoys and those the child dislikes. 2. Caregivers will describe the child's reaction to the presentation and removal of specific people, objects, and activities.

Module 3: Establishing Predictable Routines

Goal	Objectives
Caregivers will create a daily routine that includes several predictable events that the child can anticipate through recognition of certain cues such as sounds, sights, or other sensations.	1. Caregivers will identify at least five daily activities that can be scheduled in the same sequence each day. 2. Caregivers will identify predictable sequences within specific activities, or *subroutines*. 3. Caregivers will identify specific auditory, visual, tactile, olfactory, and kinesthetic cues that can be used to help the child anticipate familiar activities and daily events.

Module 4: Establishing Turn Taking

Goal	Objectives
The child will participate in familiar turn-taking routines in which he or she can interact easily with caregivers.	1. Using information gained in previous modules, caregivers will learn how to encourage the child to request more of a desired food or event. 2. Caregivers will identify and extend any current turn-taking routines and create new turn-taking games through initiation. 3. Caregivers will generalize turn-taking games across people and settings.

Module 5: Encouraging Communicative Initiations

Goal	Objectives
The child will increase his or her rate of initiations for the purposes of obtaining a desired object or pleasurable event and expressing rejection.	1. Caregivers will learn how to increase the child's initiations by encouraging the child to express rejection of a disliked object or activity. 2. Caregivers will learn to increase the child's initiations by delaying an anticipated event. 3. Caregivers will learn how to encourage the child to initiate intentionally and to obtain the caregiver's attention.

Module 1: Understanding Your Child's Cues

Goal	Recording Sheets for Each Objective
Caregivers will have a detailed picture of the ways in which the child expresses attention and interest; internal states, such as pleasure and discomfort; and needs and desires.	1. Recording Sheet 1-A: Typical Daily Activities 2. Recording Sheet 1-B: Categories of States of Arousal 3. Recording Sheet 1-C: Observations of Your Child's Responses to Daily Activities. Use information from Recording Sheet 1-A to develop a more detailed understanding of the child's reactions. 4. Recording Sheet 1-D: Your Child's Strategies and Purposes for Getting Attention 5. Update information on the *Caregiver Interview*.

Module 2: Identifying Your Child's Preferences

Goal	Recording Sheets for Each Objective
Caregivers will develop a thorough understanding of what the child enjoys and what he or she dislikes.	1. Recording Sheet 2-A: Your Child's Preferences Use information from Recording Sheet 1-A: Typical Daily Activities. 2. Recording Sheet 2-B: Your Child's Responses to People, Objects, and Activities

Module 3: Establishing Predictable Routines

Goal	Recording Sheets for Each Objective
Caregivers will create a daily routine that includes several predictable events that the child can anticipate through recognition of certain cues such as sounds, sights, or other sensations.	1. Recording Sheet 3-A: Predictable Daily Activities Use information from Recording Sheet 1-A: Typical Daily Activities. 2. Recording Sheet 3-B: Subroutines and Cues Use information gathered about the child's learning style and needs. 3. Recording Sheet 3-C: Effectiveness of New Cues Use information gathered about the child's learning style and needs. Refer to Recording Sheet 3-B: Subroutines and Cues.

Module 4: Establishing Turn Taking

Goal	Recording Sheets for Each Objective
The child will participate in familiar turn-taking routines in which he or she can interact easily with caregivers.	1. Recording Sheet 4-A: Request for More: Interruption Plans Use information from Recording Sheet 2-A: Your Child's Preferences 2. Recording Sheet 4-B: Developing Turn-Taking Games 3. Recording Sheet 4-C: Generalizing Turn-Taking Games

Module 5: Encouraging Communicative Initiations

Goal	Recording Sheets for Each Objective
The child will increase his or her rate of initiations for the purposes of obtaining a desired object or pleasurable event and expressing rejection.	1. Recording Sheet 5-A: Rejecting a Disliked Object or Activity Use information from Recording Sheet 2-A: Your Child's Preferences. 2. Recording Sheet 5-B: Increasing Initiation Use information from Recording Sheet 3-A: Predictable Daily Activities, Recording Sheet 4-A: Request for More: Interruption Plans, or Recording Sheet 4-B: Developing Turn-Taking Games. 3. Recording Sheet 5-C: Initiating Attention

Important Questions

Before filling out the *Caregiver Interview*, the service provider should already know some of the answers to several key questions about the child's vision, hearing, motor skills, and overall health. This information should be found by using multiple data sources such as available reports, caregiver interviews, and consultation with other service providers and relevant professionals who have had previous experience with the child.

Vision

1. How does this child use his or her vision? How much time does the child need to respond to a visual stimulus? What does he or she like to look at? What does he or she seem to recognize visually?
2. When was the last time that this child had his or her eyes checked? Who did this examination?
3. Does this child have a visual impairment? If yes, what is the type and degree of vision loss?
4. Does this child wear corrective lenses? Who is the child's optometrist or ophthalmologist?
5. Is this child receiving services from a teacher credentialed in the area of visual impairment?

Hearing

1. How does this child use his or her hearing? How much time does the child need to respond to sound? What does he or she seem to listen to? What sounds does he or she seem to recognize? What words does he or she seem to understand?
2. When was the last time that this child had his or her hearing checked? Who did this evaluation?
3. Does this child have a hearing impairment? If yes, what is the type and degree of hearing loss?
4. Does this child wear hearing aids? Who is the audiologist?

Motor Skills

1. How does he or she grasp, hold, or handle toys and objects?
2. Is he or she sitting, standing, or walking without help?
3. Does this child have a motor disorder? If yes, what is it? Is it progressive?
4. Is there a physical therapist or occupational therapist involved with him or her?
5. Is this child receiving services from a teacher accredited in the area of hearing impairment?

Health

1. How would you describe the child's health?
2. If this child has medical problems, what are they?
3. Is this child taking any medication? If yes, what medication? What is it used to treat? Are there any side effects?

Summary

1. What are the child's main strengths?
2. In what situations does this child seem to be the most attentive and responsive?
3. What are this child's primary needs?
4. What current services is this child receiving?

PLAI CAREGIVER INTERVIEW

Child's name _____ Date of birth _____

Caregiver's name _____ Relationship to child _____

Interviewer's name _____ Date of interview _____

The first step to improving your child's communication skills is to see ways that your child can already communicate and how often that communication occurs. Please record the behavior that you have observed in as much detail as you can. This interview has several sections. Please complete all sections.

Section One—Your Child's Feelings		
Feeling	**How do you know?**	**In what situations?**
Hungry		
Uncomfortable		
Surprised or startled		
Happy		
Sad		
Angry		
Tired		
Scared		
Overstimulated		
Frustrated (becomes upset during activities)		
Wants "more" of something (e.g., food, a person or activity)		
Wants to end an activity		
Wants interaction		
Wants to be left alone		

PLAI: A Guide to Early Communication with Young Children Who Have Multiple Disabilities © 2000 by Paul H. Brookes Publishing Co.

Section Two—Your Child's Behaviors					
Behavior	**When does it happen?**	**How often?** 1=Never/rarely 2=Sometimes 3=Frequently		
Makes expressions (e.g., smiles, frowns)		1	2	3
Laughs		1	2	3
Cries		1	2	3
Screams (can be calmed)		1	2	3
Tantrums (cannot be calmed)		1	2	3
Looks at people		1	2	3
Looks at or touches objects		1	2	3
Moves body (e.g., leans forward)		1	2	3
Moves head to look at a person or object		1	2	3
Moves head to hear a sound better		1	2	3
Points to or reaches for a person or object		1	2	3
Imitates others' actions		1	2	3
Gestures with arms or hands		1	2	3
Makes sounds (nonspeech-like)		1	2	3
Babbles (speech-like)		1	2	3
Signs or says single words		1	2	3
Other (describe)		1	2	3

PLAI: A Guide to Early Communication with Young Children Who Have Multiple Disabilities © 2000 by Paul H. Brookes Publishing Co.

Section Three—Cues	
Type of cue	Describe the cue
Tactile cues (e.g., placing your child's hands in the water before a bath; touching your child's lips to signal "eat")	
Object cues (e.g., allowing your child to handle the blanket in which you are about to swing him or her)	
Auditory cues (e.g., squeaking a toy near your child's ear before you give it to him or her)	
Kinesthetic cues (e.g., rocking your child in your arms before you start swinging him or her)	
Olfactory cues (e.g., giving your child a smell of the shampoo before washing his or her hair)	
Visual cues (e.g., showing your child the bathtub before a bath)	

PLAI: A Guide to Early Communication with Young Children Who Have Multiple Disabilities © 2000 by Paul H. Brookes Publishing Co.

Section Four—Your Child's Preferences

1. Does your child ever indicate a choice between two objects (e.g., preferring milk instead of juice or a rocker instead of a swing)? Think about a situation or specific daily activity like playtime. If you offer two toys, does your child make a choice? When there are people in the room (including yourself), does your child reach or make some kind of signal to you? If yes, how?

2. Are there situations in which your child must gain your attention in order to get some desired object or to meet a particular need? Does your child initiate communication intentionally? When you are talking to other people or paying attention to something else, will your child try to get your attention? If yes, when?

3. Is there a special way that your child responds to you that is different than the way he or she responds to other people?

4. In what ways do you soothe or comfort your child when she or he is upset? Please explain.

5. Are there any games (e.g., Peekaboo, Pat-a-Cake) that your child enjoys? Please explain.

6. When is your child most communicative (e.g., some children vocalize, reach for things, or smile more during physical movement activities; other children are more interactive when they are being fed)?

PLAI: A Guide to Early Communication with Young Children Who Have Multiple Disabilities © 2000 by Paul H. Brookes Publishing Co.

Case Study: Michael's Story

Michael is 14 months old. We will be following Michael's mother, Cecelia, and his older sister, Kate, as they learn about PLAI. Michael was born very prematurely, at 26 weeks. He weighed only 1 pound 8 ounces at birth, and he was on a respirator for nearly 2 months. He had numerous complications and medical procedures while he was in the neonatal intensive care unit including an intraventricular hemorrhage. When he was discharged from the hospital he was diagnosed with multiple disabilities, including severe retinopathy of prematurity (ROP), increased muscle tone indicative of spastic cerebral palsy, and an undetermined degree of hearing loss.

During Michael's first year, his development was very slow. He was an irritable baby, and feeding was very difficult, although that was the one area where there had definitely been improvement. He is now able to use a special nipple and take up to 6 ounces of a special formula.

MODULE 1: Understanding Your Child's Cues

Cecelia's daily schedule was initially fairly unpredictable. She would sometimes help out in her uncle's bakery when they were shorthanded. Usually, this was in the late afternoon or evening when Kate was available to stay with Michael. And Cecelia would often babysit for her sister's children when her sister had problems finding child care.

The most predictable events occurred early in the morning and late at night. Because of Kate's school schedule, the family got up at about 6 A.M. every morning. Cecelia would fix Kate's breakfast, then get Michael out of bed and give him his bottle. After Kate left for school, Cecelia would give Michael a bath and dress him. For the rest of the day, the schedule was unpredictable, until nighttime. Kate or Cecelia gave Michael his nighttime bottle. Sometimes Kate rocked him to sleep while watching TV.

When asked to think about the last objective of Module 1, they were much surer of how Michael expressed pleasure and interest: He extended his arms and legs slightly, moved his head to midline and down, and became very still. They also learned to recognize that he was becoming upset before he actually started to cry: He would pull his head up at midline, hyperextend his legs, and clench his fists.

As Cecelia began to observe Michael's reactions to familiar daily activities, she realized that when she went to lift him out of his crib, even before she said anything to him, he would extend his arms and legs. She wondered how he could sense her presence. Maybe he could smell her. At first, she thought maybe it was her imagination; but as she observed several times and used Recording Sheet 1-C: Observations of Your Child's Responses to Daily Activities, she realized that his response was consistent. He would always respond as she approached the crib. She also discovered another thing. At night, if Kate gave him his bottle, he had a much harder time settling into a good sucking rhythm, and he seemed to spit up more. When Cecelia gave him his bottle, this rarely happened. Cecelia told the service provider that she had mixed feelings about this. She really wanted Kate to love Michael, so she didn't mention this discovery to Kate for fear that it would hurt her feelings. But at the same time she had to admit that it felt good to realize how tuned in Michael was to her presence and that he really seemed to know she was someone special.

After the discovery that Michael responded consistently by extending his arms and legs when she approached his crib, Cecelia and Kate became anxious to work on the third objective of Module 1 to see if they could discover other things they hadn't known about Michael. The service provider helped Kate and Cecelia notice that when Michael (sitting in his infant seat) was in a drowsy or tuned out state, his head would usually be turned to the side and slightly down. When he was alert and paying attention to something, he would extend his arms and legs a bit, and move his head more toward midline, though his head would still be down. Cecelia said that even though she knew Michael could not see, it was hard for her to realize that he could be paying attention when his head was down. As she continued to observe him carefully, she also discovered that when his head was up, he was actually becoming upset and overaroused. As he became more tense, he would hold his head up momentarily but then begin to fuss and cry shortly thereafter.

Cecelia discovered another response. When she massaged his fingers, which she had always assumed he liked, his head would come up, and his fists would clench slightly. But when she massaged his shoulders and upper back, his fists would relax, and his head would turn to midline and down. She realized that he loved having this part of his body touched but that his hands were fairly hypersensitive.

Cecelia had been very aware that Michael did not do things to try to get her attention, and this had made her feel that Michael barely knew she existed. When the service provider discussed the fourth objective of Module 1 with her, she told her that it might be quite a while before Michael tried to get her attention and that learning how to do this often took much longer for a baby with disabilities. After working on these objectives in Module 1, Kate and Cecelia felt they knew Michael better.

MODULE 2: Identifying Your Child's Preferences

After this period of observing and learning more about Michael's cues, Cecelia and Kate could easily complete Recording Sheet 2-A: Your Child's Preferences. Michael's favorite things were his mom, cinnamon rolls, shoulder massages, and rocking in Kate's lap. He really hated citrus fruits, being naked, and being immersed in water. He also had a moderate aversion to having his hands touched and to sudden loud noises. Because of the discovery of Michael's reaction to certain noises, the service provider suggested that it might be a good time to schedule another hearing test in the hopes of getting a clearer picture of the status of his hearing and considering the possibility of a hearing aid.

Kate was particularly enthusiastic about this new project of discovering Michael's preferences and was very creative about presenting various objects and experiences to Michael to see how he would respond. It was Kate who discovered that Michael had a particularly good sense of smell and that he loved certain smells and hated others. His favorite seemed to be the smell of cinnamon rolls that Cecelia would sometimes bring home from the bakery. Kate could even get him to stop fussing by putting the cinnamon roll under his nose, then putting a little taste of the cinnamon and sugar in his mouth. She also discovered that he had a strong aversion to several fruits, such as oranges and lemons. The smell or taste of these would make him throw his head back and begin to cry.

MODULE 3: Establishing Predictable Routines

In Module 3, Cecelia had the opportunity to think about her family's daily schedule. Her service provider helped her realize how it could help Michael if his daily events were more predictable, that he would feel safer and more "in control," and that it would help him better understand what was going on around him.

In addition to the morning routine of getting Michael out of the crib and giving him his bottle, Cecelia decided to try to increase the predictability of their daily routine in the following ways:
- After Michael finished his bottle, she would consistently give him his bath.
- After his bath, she would put lotion on him and give him a shoulder and back massage.

Even if there was very little time, Cecelia said she would do it for at least a minute or two.

At bedtime, Cecelia would generally give him his bottle, and then Kate would rock him while watching TV. This would make the morning activities and the bedtime activities fairly predictable. After working on the next objective of identifying subroutines, Cecelia realized that she and Michael had already established a subroutine. This occurred during diapering. After taking off the diaper and washing Michael's bottom, Cecelia would blow on Michael's tummy a couple of times, saying, "Okay, all dry, all dry." Then she would sprinkle a little baby powder (Michael seemed to like the smell of the powder), put the diaper on and say, "All done." Then she would give him a kiss while picking him up.

In the third objective, Cecelia learned that she could help Michael even more by adding certain consistent sensory cues to her daily activities and subroutines. She and Kate decided on the following cues:

- Before going into his room to take him out of the crib, Cecelia would always say, "Here comes Mommy" in a fairly loud voice. Then she would put her hands on his shoulders before picking him up.
- Before putting him in the bath, she would put his foot in the water a couple of times.
- Before giving him his back massage, she would rub some of the lotion on her fingers and let Michael smell it.
- During diapering, she would let him smell the powder before she sprinkled it, and she would touch the diaper to his hand before putting it on him.

Although Cecelia was very enthusiastic initially about these procedures, she found it was much harder to remember to do them than she expected. Also, she couldn't really see any effect on Michael. She wasn't sure what the point was, although she did notice that within only a week of starting the "foot in the water" cue at bath time, Michael stopped screaming when she put him in the bathtub. But none of the other cues seemed to have much effect on Michael. Cecelia didn't do them consistently. She remembered only about half the time. Her service provider told her not to get discouraged and that it might take several months before she would see any anticipation in Michael.

Cecelia continued and really made an effort to be more consistent. After about four months, she did notice an interesting thing. Sometimes when she let Michael smell the lotion, he would get an odd expression on his face, and sometimes she thought it almost looked like a smile. This made sense because he really loved his back and shoulder massages. Michael rarely smiled and when he did, it was never clear what he was smiling about. This "almost smile" in anticipation of his back rub made Cecelia realize how much she longed to see Michael smile at her. Although her service provider had explained that this type of social smile was often significantly delayed in children like Michael, it didn't make Cecelia want it any less.

MODULE 4: Establishing Turn Taking

Module 4 was a turning point. In the first three modules, Cecelia had focused on observing Michael and on creating a more predictable environment and using more consistent cues. Now the emphasis was really on helping Michael learn some new behaviors. The first objective helped Cecelia and Kate teach Michael to request more of something he liked. This was easy to do with the cinnamon and sugar icing from the cinnamon roll. Kate would let him smell it, then give him a taste with her finger. Normally she would touch his lips, and he would open his mouth. In this objective, she learned that if she simply waited after giving him the first taste, he would eventually open his mouth and bring his head to midline. Kate would then say, "Oh, you want another taste, don't you!" and give him a taste.

Cecelia also used this strategy whenever she gave Michael a backrub. After massaging his back and shoulders for about 30 seconds, she would stop and wait. Usually within about 10–15 seconds, Michael would lift his head and extend his arms slightly, indicating he wanted more.

The goal of this module is to help your child learn to participate in turn-taking games, like Peekaboo. The service provider explained to Cecelia that it is very difficult for children who have hearing and vision problems and other severe disabilities to learn these social games. Cecelia noted that Michael really never did this. So they decided to try one of the strategies in Module 4 to work on this. Cecelia used the "request for more" they had already established in the lotion and massage routine. She simply shortened the massage to 2–3 seconds, waited for Michael to extend his arms, did it for 2–3 more seconds, then waited again. She was worried that this would be irritating and frustrating to him. But surprisingly, he seemed to catch on that they were now playing a game. Cecelia commented that now he seems to enjoy the game aspect of it as much as he enjoys actual-

PLAI: A Guide to Early Communication with Young Children Who Have Multiple Disabilities ©2000 by Paul H. Brookes Publishing Co.

ly getting the back rub. What's even better, this is the one situation where Michael will now consistently smile!

Next, Cecelia taught Kate how to play this game. Michael quickly understood that he could play this game with Kate as well as with Mom. Cecelia also tried to generalize the game to Michael's service provider. Michael seemed more hesitant about this, maybe because they were doing the massage at the wrong time of day, as well as doing it with someone who didn't normally perform this function. Cecelia thinks Michael will first have to get used to the service provider giving him a massage before he will be interested in playing the turn-taking game with her.

MODULE 5: Encouraging Communicative Initiations

Cecelia and Kate tried to get Michael to use some kind of clear signal of rejection for oranges and grapefruit, which he hates. This effort was not successful because his signals were very inconsistent.

The second objective of increasing initiations was more successful. They decided to delay one of Michael's most anticipated events: rocking with Kate before bedtime. After Cecelia finished giving him his bottle, Kate would take Michael and sit in the rocking chair and turn on the TV. But instead of immediately starting to rock, Kate would simply sit there, not moving. At first, Michael made no response at all. He got very quiet and still as though trying to figure out what was wrong. Then he would extend his arms and legs and raise his head up as he typically does when he's getting upset. As soon as he moved his arms, Kate would say, "Do you want me to rock?" and she would start rocking him. In this situation, Michael was learning to initiate and request that something start, not simply a request for more of something that was already ongoing and had been interrupted.

The last objective in this module proved to be much more difficult. The goal of this objective was to teach Michael to signal for attention even when Cecelia was not in close proximity. Because Michael was starting to vocalize more, she tried to get him to vocalize to get her to come to him when she was not in the same room. Whenever Michael was left alone in his infant seat, Cecelia would listen for him to vocalize. As soon as he did, she would go into the room and say, "Here I am, Michael. In just a minute I'll pick you up." However, his rate of vocalizing did not seem to increase. More often than not, when Michael thought he had been left alone, he would get agitated and start to cry.

Michael was still not really initiating to get someone's attention, and they would continue to work on this goal. Nevertheless, Michael and Cecelia had both changed in some very important ways since they first started the curriculum. Cecelia felt that she understood Michael much better. She was much more aware of his likes and dislikes, and she was better able to read his signals. She was much more consistent in how she interacted with Michael and more patient. Except when she was under a lot of stress, Cecelia would give Michael plenty of time to respond. Michael was also changing. He was much clearer in his communication behaviors. He seemed to be more purposefully communicating with Cecelia and Kate, he was starting to vocalize more, he spent more time in an awake and alert state, and he would even smile.

Module 1

Handouts

Module 1 Overview

Recording Sheet 1-A: Typical Daily Activities

Recording Sheet 1-B: Categories of States of Arousal

Situations, Antecedents, Behaviors, and Consequences

Recording Sheet 1-C: Observations of Your Child's Responses to Daily Activities

Recording Sheet 1-D: Your Child's Strategies and Purposes for Getting Attention

Module 1 Summary

Overview of Module 1: Understanding Your Child's Cues

Rationale	Children communicate in many ways, long before they begin to talk. When you respond and correctly interpret these early communications (e.g., facial expressions, sounds, pointing), it helps your child to understand language and encourages him or her to communicate even more. When children have multiple disabilities (e.g., severe developmental delays, hearing loss, visual impairment, difficulties with physical movement, or medical needs), their communication signals are often hard to recognize and understand. Before you can help your child to learn new ways of communicating, you must first discover the ways your child is currently communicating, as well as the kinds of things about which your child is most motivated to communicate.
Goal	The goal of Module 1 is to help you become a very careful observer of your child's cues (i.e., signals that communicate your child's feelings and desires). At the end of Module 1, you will have a very detailed picture of how your child expresses attention and interest, as well as what we call "state of arousal" (i.e., alert, sleepy, content, upset) and how he or she responds to changes in the environment.
Activities	Several activities have been designed to help you practice these observation skills and identify all the ways in which your child communicates. You will begin by taking a closer look at your child's daily activities. Through a series of careful observations focused on your child's typical day, you can keep track of his or her responses to the people and activities in the daily environment. Forms are provided to help you record communicative behaviors that can be difficult to recognize and might otherwise be easily overlooked.

PLAI: A Guide to Early Communication with Young Children Who Have Multiple Disabilities ©2000 by Paul H. Brookes Publishing Co.

Recording Sheet 1-A

Date_____ Child's name_____ Observer's name_____

Typical Daily Activities

Time	Activity	Likes	Dislikes	How do you know?
6–7 A.M.				
7–8 A.M.				
8–9 A.M.				
9–10 A.M.				
10–11 A.M.				
11–12 P.M.				
12–1 P.M.				
1–2 P.M.				
2–3 P.M.				
3–4 P.M.				
4–5 P.M.				
5–6 P.M.				
6–7 P.M.				
7–8 P.M.				
8–9 P.M.				
9–10 P.M.				
10–11 P.M.				

PLAI: A Guide to Early Communication with Young Children Who Have Multiple Disabilities ©2000 by Paul H. Brookes Publishing Co.

Recording Sheet 1-B

Date_____ Child's name_____ Observer's name_____

Categories of States of Arousal

State	Description
Active and alert	Your child attempts to engage or interact with other people (e.g., looks at mother's face, vocalizes) or with the environment (e.g., reaches for a toy, bangs the table) using vision, hearing, sounds, or touch.
Crying or agitated	Your child vocalizes intensely, cries, or screams. Your child may grimace or frown with or without intense vocalization and may have increased body tension or intense movement.
Dazed or tuned out	Your child is awake but doesn't pay attention to sights, sounds, or touches. Your child's eyes may appear glassy or dull. He or she may move limbs or body a little or startle slightly.
Drowsy	Your child's eyes are open but eyelids appear heavy; or your child's eyes may open and close repeated. He or she may vocalize.
Engaging in repetitive or stereotypical behavior	Your child is actively engaged in movements that are stereotypical, repetitive, or rhythmic (e.g., head weaving, waving arms, sucking or mouthing, rocking, hand flapping).
Fussy or irritable	Your child's sounds or facial expressions have a complaining or uncomfortable quality, but he or she is not yet crying.
Quiet and alert	Your child's eyes are open, and there is some focusing on sights, sounds, or touches. Your child may move his or her limbs or body a little or startle slightly.

Which of these states have you observed in your child?

State	When

PLAI: A Guide to Early Communication with Young Children Who Have Multiple Disabilities ©2000 by Paul H. Brookes Publishing Co.

Situations, Antecedents, Behaviors, and Consequences

This chart can help you recognize antecedents, behaviors, and consequences with your own child. It can also help you fill out Recording Sheet 1-C. This example shows possible antecedents, behaviors, and consequences for bath time, an everyday activity. It is important to notice that a behavior is connected to what happens before it. Sometimes, if you change the antecedent, you can change the behavior.

Situation (What is happening?)
Bath time

Antecedent (What happens just before the child's behavior?)	**Behavior** (What does the child do?)	**Consequence** (How does the caregiver respond to the child's behavior?)
Mom undresses Joey and puts him in the bath.	Joey arches his back and cries.	Mom changes his position.
Mom dips his toes in the water, then puts him in the bath.	Joey grimaces.	Mom talks to him.
Mom says, "Bath time!" and puts him in the bath.	Joey whimpers a little.	Mom soothes him.
Mom begins to wash Joey's face and hair.	Joey screams.	Mom sings to him.
Mom puts the shampoo bottle under Joey's nose.	Joey becomes quiet and alert.	Mom talks to him.

PLAI: A Guide to Early Communication with Young Children Who Have Multiple Disabilities ©2000 by Paul H. Brookes Publishing Co.

Recording Sheet 1-C

Child's name _____ Observer's name _____ Date _____

Observations of Your Child's Responses to Daily Activities

First fill in the situation and behavior sections, then reflect on the antecedents and consequences of your child's behavior.

Situation (What is happening?)	Antecedent (What happens just before your child's behavior?)	Behavior (What does your child do?)	Consequence (How do you respond to your child's behavior?)

PLAI: A Guide to Early Communication with Young Children Who Have Multiple Disabilities ©2000 by Paul H. Brookes Publishing Co.

Recording Sheet 1-D

Child's name _____ Observer's name _____

Your Child's Strategies and Purposes for Getting Attention

Describe a situation in which your child was trying to get your attention.	How did your child get your attention?	What do you think your child was trying to communicate?	Date observed

PLAI: A Guide to Early Communication with Young Children Who Have Multiple Disabilities ©2000 by Paul H. Brookes Publishing Co.

Module 1 Summary

Child's name _____ Date _____

This recording sheet can help you summarize what you've learned about your child by completing the objectives in Module 1. Please share this information with your child's teachers and other caregivers.

Understanding Your Child's Cues
1. Our daily schedule includes the following regularly occurring activities   _____   _____   _____   _____   _____   _____   2. My child's favorite time of day is _____   3. My child communicates in the following ways   _____   _____   _____   4. The reasons why my child usually communicates are   _____   _____   _____   _____   _____   _____   5. My child gets my attention by   _____   _____   _____   _____

PLAI: A Guide to Early Communication with Young Children Who Have Multiple Disabilities ©2000 by Paul H. Brookes Publishing Co.

Module 2

Handouts

Module 2 Overview

Recording Sheet 2-A: Your Child's Preferences

Recording Sheet 2-B: Your Child's Responses to People, Objects, and Activities

Module 2 Summary

Overview of Module 2: Identifying Your Child's Preferences

Rationale	Motivation is the key to any kind of learning. Knowing your child's likes and dislikes for different objects, people, foods, and activities is very useful. Your child's likes and dislikes can be used in motivating him or her to communicate to obtain or reject these things. Now that you have completed the observations in Module 1, it is simple to identify your child's least and most favorite things. Later, in Module 4, you will learn some simple strategies for using these things to teach your child new ways to communicate.
Goal	The goal of Module 2 is to develop a list of preferences. This list will need to be updated periodically over time because preferences will change as your child matures.
Activities	The activities for Module 2 are simple. You will list the people, objects, and activities that your child likes, identifying which of those he or she especially loves and which of those he or she really hates! You will take a careful look at your child's responses to certain people, objects, and activities when they are presented and when they are removed.

PLAI: A Guide to Early Communication with Young Children Who Have Multiple Disabilities ©2000 by Paul H. Brookes Publishing Co.

Recording Sheet 2-A

Child's name _____ Observer's name _____ Date _____

Your Child's Preferences

	Really Likes	Likes	Dislikes	Really Dislikes
People				
Objects				
Activities				

PLAI: A Guide to Early Communication with Young Children Who Have Multiple Disabilities ©2000 by Paul H. Brookes Publishing Co.

Recording Sheet 2-B

Date_____ Child's name_____ Observer's name_____

Your Child's Responses to People, Objects, and Activities

Before filling this out, refer to Recording Sheet 1-B for descriptions of states. Note that it is not necessary to present and take away each person, object, or event. Review your completed sheet to identify 1) differences in your child's responses in different states, 2) differences in your child's reactions to familiar and new experiences, 3) differences in your child's responses to removal and presentation, 4) what your child likes and dislikes, and 5) how your child demonstrates these likes and dislikes.

N = a new person, object, or event   F = a familiar person, object, or event

State	What did you present?	How did your child respond to this?	N	F

State	What did you take away?	How did your child respond to this?	N	F

PLAI: A Guide to Early Communication with Young Children Who Have Multiple Disabilities ©2000 by Paul H. Brookes Publishing Co.

Module 2 Summary

Child's name _____ Date _____

This recording sheet can help you summarize what you've learned about your child by completing the objective in Module 2. Please share this information with your child's teachers and other caregivers.

Identifying Your Child's Preferences
1. My child's favorite things are People _____ _____ _____ _____ _____ _____ Objects _____ _____ _____ _____ _____ _____ Activities _____ _____ _____ _____ _____ _____ 2. My child really dislikes these People _____ _____ _____ _____ Objects _____ _____ _____ _____ Activities _____ _____ _____ _____

PLAI: A Guide to Early Communication with Young Children Who Have Multiple Disabilities ©2000 by Paul H. Brookes Publishing Co.

Module 3

Handouts

Module 3 Overview

Recording Sheet 3-A: Predictable Daily Activities

Recording Sheet 3-B: Subroutines and Cues

Tactile Cues

Auditory Cues

Kinesthetic Cues

Olfactory Cues

Visual Cues

Recording Sheet 3-C: Effectiveness of New Cues

Module 3 Summary

Overview of Module 3: Establishing Predictable Routines

Rationale	One of the things that helps children understand the world around them is having a predictable schedule. By identifying frequently occurring activities and establishing a consistent order in which they will occur each day, you can create for your child a sense of confidence and control over his or her environment. Your child will begin to understand what is about to happen by recognizing certain cues and signals that occur just prior to the familiar activity or event (e.g., getting undressed and playing Pat-a-cake before taking a bath). *Subroutines* are also important. These are consistent sequences or steps that occur within a familiar activity like bath time or dressing. Once these routines are established, the consistent pairing of certain words, sights, and touch sensations with each activity (e.g., always helping your child feel the running water before placing him or her in the bathtub) will eventually give meaning to those words or other cues. Making the most of your child's senses will increase his or her ability to anticipate familiar activities and daily events. Consistent use of these cues will also help your child increase his or her attentional focus and eventually will make it easier for you and your child to establish joint attention to a single object or activity.
Goal	There are three goals in Module 3. The first is to establish certain predictable events within your daily schedule (e.g., always rocking your child after lunch and before naptime). The second is to identify or establish certain subroutines within frequently occurring activities (e.g., always following the same steps and using the same words when changing your child's diaper). The third goal is to make maximum use of your child's senses to help him or her anticipate and understand these predictable events (e.g., always touching the back of his or her hand with the washcloth before washing his or her face).
Activities	Using Recording Sheet 1-A: Typical Daily Activities, you will identify the most predictable events in your daily routine. You may wish to increase the predictability of your daily schedule. You will also describe the specific steps of any existing subroutines that you use. Or you may wish to create one or two new subroutines that you think might be fun for both you and your child. In this module, you also may work on identifying ways of making greater use of your child's senses to help him or her anticipate and understand an activity.

PLAI: A Guide to Early Communication with Young Children Who Have Multiple Disabilities ©2000 by Paul H. Brookes Publishing Co.

Recording Sheet 3-A

Child's name _____ Observer's name _____

Predictable Daily Activities

First fill in the daily activity, then note the approximate time and what happens before and after the activity.

What usually happens before?	Daily activity	Approximate time	What usually happens after?

PLAI: A Guide to Early Communication with Young Children Who Have Multiple Disabilities ©2000 by Paul H. Brookes Publishing Co.

Recording Sheet 3-B

Child's name _____ Observer's name _____

Subroutines and Cues

Use a separate recording sheet for each activity.

Activity

Subroutine	Cues I usually use	New cues to add

PLAI: A Guide to Early Communication with Young Children Who Have Multiple Disabilities ©2000 by Paul H. Brookes Publishing Co.

Tactile Cues

Tactile cues involve touching your child in a specific way to let him or her know what is about to happen. They are very helpful for communicating with young children who have severe physical disabilities and developmental delays or severe visual impairments and hearing loss.

Touch cues should be precise, perceivable, and pleasant for the child in order to support attention and anticipation of an activity. Use one touch cue at a time. It will be more difficult for a child with severe disabilities to learn the exact meaning of a touch cue if more than one touch cue is used in a single activity or if the cue occurs simultaneously with touching the child during physical handling and interaction. Certain types of touch on specific body areas may elict reflex movements in some children with motor or neurological impairments.

Other young children with medical needs dislike being touched on the bottom of the foot because of their experience with medical interventions. In general, a firm or deep pressure touch is more easily tolerated than a light, feathery stroke. However, the type of touch and placement of each touch cue should be selected carefully for the individual child, then used systematically.

Here are some touch cues that may work for your child:

- Before washing your child's face, stroke his or her cheek.
- Before giving your child a drink from a cup, hold his or her chin.
- Tap your child's lips twice with your fingers before giving him or her the first bite of food.

Here is a manual cue that may work for your child:

- Before giving your child a bite of food, physically guide him or her to sign the word EAT (i.e., sign coactively).

Here are some object cues that may work for your child:

- Touch the washcloth to your child's hand before putting him or her into the bath tub.
- When dressing your child, touch the shirt to your child's chest before putting it on him or her.

PLAI: A Guide to Early Communication with Young Children Who Have Multiple Disabilities ©2000 by Paul H. Brookes Publishing Co.

Auditory Cues

Sound cues are a natural way to get a child's attention. At first, most children tend to be more responsive to rhythmic sound or exaggerated intonation.

In order for the child to make use of sounds as meaningful cues, background noise (i.e., television, radio, and other distracting environmental sounds) should be eliminated as much as possible so that the child can focus on the auditory cues.

Some kinds of sounds may be irritating to a particular child. For example, some children with disabilities are extremely sensitive and may overreact to any increase in loudness. Also, sudden bursts of sound may cause a child to startle and even cry. Some environments cause sound reverberation that may be irritating and may make it more difficult for the child who has hearing loss or auditory processing disorder to attend to and localize specific sounds. Generally, this occurs in rooms with little sound-absorbing material. For example, a kitchen with a tile floor and no curtains would be a much more resonant noise environment than a living room with carpet, curtains, and overstuffed furniture. Many children who have a hearing loss have some residual hearing and can perceive some sounds.

Here are some sound cues that may work for your child:

- Clink the spoon on the side of the bowl before giving your child a bite.
- Gently tap the cup on the table before giving your child a drink.
- Sing a few lines of the theme song of your child's favorite television show before turning on the television.
- Shake your child's bottle of milk near his or her head before putting the nipple to his or her mouth.

Here are some word cues that may work for your child:

- Say your child's name when you are about to present something to him or her, when you are about to interact with him or her, or when you are about to greet him or her.
- In simple language, tell your child what you are about to do (e.g., "Mama's going to wash your face now.").
- Use single key words as cues (e.g., "wash," "dinner").

PLAI: A Guide to Early Communication with Young Children Who Have Multiple Disabilities ©2000 by Paul H. Brookes Publishing Co.

Kinesthetic Cues

Kinesthetic or movement cues are actually combinations of movement and tactile sensation. They involve handling, positioning, and moving your child in certain ways associated with the upcoming activity. If a child has cerebral palsy, kinesthetic cues should be selected with consideration for the child's muscle tone. Children with low tone (hypotonia) tend to mold easily when held but may be difficult to arouse. They usually benefit from physical stimulation, handling, and positioning that increase muscle tone and arouse attention. Children with high tone (hypertonia) may be irritable and difficult to hold. Specific positioning and careful handling will be needed to reduce tone and improve the quality, amount, and range of the child's movements. Do not use kinesthetic cues that elicit reflexive or involuntary movements (e.g., if turning the child's head to one side causes the child's legs and arms to move in the same direction or if swinging the child without proper positioning and support triggers trunk and limb extension). In general, hold and support your child while moving him or her so that he or she can maintain a symmetrical and flexed body position.

Here are some whole body movement cues that may work for your child:

- Before sitting down to rock your child in a rocking chair, rock back and forth while holding him or her at your shoulder.
- Hold your child away from your body, and gently swing him or her before putting your child in an infant swing.

Here are some limb movement cues that may work for your child:

- Before lifting your child out of the highchair, lift up slightly on his or her elbows.
- Lift your child's arms above his or her head before taking his or her shirt off.
- Clap your child's hands together once before playing Pat-a-cake.

PLAI: A Guide to Early Communication with Young Children Who Have Multiple Disabilities ©2000 by Paul H. Brookes Publishing Co.

Olfactory Cues

Smells associated with objects and people can be used as olfactory cues. Your child may anticipate that you are going to pick him or her up if you always wear the same cologne. Some children may be very sensitive to certain smells, yet other children may not seem to notice them. Carefully observe your child's preferences and responses to smells. Some children are extremely sensitive to cologne and other strong odors. You will need to observe carefully to determine whether certain odors produce overstimulation or a negative reaction from your child.

Here are some smell cues that may work for your child:

- Before washing your child's hair, let him or her smell the shampoo.
- Let your child smell the food in the bowl before giving him or her the first bite.
- Make it a habit to wear the same cologne on your wrists. Before picking up your child, hold your wrist close to his or her nose, then greet your child.

PLAI: A Guide to Early Communication with Young Children Who Have Multiple Disabilities ©2000 by Paul H. Brookes Publishing Co.

Visual Cues

The use of color, contrast, lighting, spacing, and arrangement can make an object more visible to children with severe disabilities. Objects can be seen more easily when they are against a solid, glare-free background of contrasting color. For example, a white bowl on a blue place mat has better contrast than a white bowl on a white highchair tray. The human face is a low-contrast visual image, so a child with visual impairment may have difficulty recognizing his or her dark-skinned, brown-haired mother who is wearing a tan blouse and is sitting in front of a wall of wood paneling. Contrast can be used to make the mother's face easier to see: The mother might put on bright lipstick, wear a blue blouse, or sit in front of a white wall.

Distracting visual objects should be reduced so that your child's visual attention can be engaged. For example, some children may be distracted from the activity if they face an open window with bright sunshine, or they will have difficulty seeing an object that is placed among other toys or on a patterned quilt. Visual cues should be presented within the child's visual field, and the child should be encouraged to look at and (when appropriate) touch the object. Systematic and consistent use of color, lighting, and contrast can assist your child in organizing visual information and in recognizing familiar situations.

Here is a lighting cue that may work for your child:

- Before beginning a familiar activity, use a flashlight in a dimly lit area to focus your child's attention on a specific object that will be used first in the activity (e.g., highlight a favorite toy, cup, or your face).

Here are some contrast cues that may work for your child:

- Before placing your child in the highchair, place a brightly colored bowl on the highchair to signal meal time.
- Before placing your child on the floor, place a colorful favorite toy on a different solid-colored quilt to indicate playtime.

Here is a color cue that may work for your child:

- Select objects in black, white, and primary colors to use as cues for daily activities (e.g., use a blue washcloth to indicate bath time, or select a yellow bottle or red cup for your child's milk).

Here is a manual cue that may work for your child:

- Use a conventional gesture or key word sign (if appropriate) to signal an activity. Make these hand movements slowly, and repeat them. Wear a solid, high contrast shirt to make your hands easy to see.

PLAI: A Guide to Early Communication with Young Children Who Have Multiple Disabilities ©2000 by Paul H. Brookes Publishing Co.

Recording Sheet 3-C

Child's name _____ Observer's name _____

Effectiveness of New Cues

Record your child's responses each time you try a new cue.

Date	Cue tried	Results

PLAI: A Guide to Early Communication with Young Children Who Have Multiple Disabilities ©2000 by Paul H. Brookes Publishing Co.

Module 3 Summary

Child's name _____ Date _____

This recording sheet can help you summarize what you've learned about your child by completing the objectives in Module 3. Please share this information with your child's teachers and other caregivers.

Establishing Predictable Routines

These are the predictable activities in my child's daily schedule.

Time	Activity

These are the activities that include consistent subroutines.

Activity	Subroutines

PLAI: A Guide to Early Communication with Young Children Who Have Multiple Disabilities ©2000 by Paul H. Brookes Publishing Co.

Module 4

Handouts

Module 4 Overview

Recording Sheet 4-A: Request for More: Interruption Plans

Recording Sheet 4-B: Developing Turn-Taking Games

Recording Sheet 4-C: Generalizing Turn-Taking Games

Module 4 Summary

Overview of Module 4: Establishing Turn Taking

Rationale	For children who do not have disabilities, one of the earliest communication routines is what is called "turn taking." Not long after a child is born, he or she begins to engage in interactions with the primary caregiver in which each partner takes a turn. For example, a mother blows on her child's tummy, then the child gurgles, kicks, and then stops. The mother blows again, and the child takes another turn, then stops and waits again. Such turn taking ensures that the caregiver and the child are engaged or connected to one another communicatively and emotionally. Such turn taking eventually evolves into games like Peekaboo and Pat-a-cake. However, for the child who has disabilities, turn taking may be very slow to develop. Module 4 will show you some ways to encourage turn-taking routines and games with your child.
Goal	The goal of Module 4 is to develop and extend turn-taking routines with your child.
Activities	The first procedure in Module 4 will be to encourage your child to request more of something by interrupting a pleasurable activity. You will identify any existing turn-taking routines that you already do with your child and try to make them last longer by extending them across more turns. You will also learn to create new turn-taking routines in two ways. The first way begins with interrupting a pleasurable activity, then extending the request for more over several turns. The second way of creating a new turn-taking activity is an imitation procedure in which you attempt to enter into an activity that the child is already doing by imitating his or her actions. These methods will encourage your child to participate in new turn-taking games.

PLAI: A Guide to Early Communication with Young Children Who Have Multiple Disabilities ©2000 by Paul H. Brookes Publishing Co.

Recording Sheet 4-A

Child's name _____ Observer's name _____

Request for More: Interruption Plans

Describe the plan for interrupting your child's favorite activities, then record the results each time you use this plan.

Plan		Results		
Favorite activity	How will you interrupt this activity?	Date tried	How did your child respond?	Comments

PLAI: A Guide to Early Communication with Young Children Who Have Multiple Disabilities ©2000 by Paul H. Brookes Publishing Co.

Recording Sheet 4-B

Child's name _____ Observer's name _____

Developing Turn-Taking Games

Describe the plan for each game, then record the results each time you play the game with your child.

Plan		Results
Favorite activity	What you will do?	Date tried	How did your child respond?

PLAI: A Guide to Early Communication with Young Children Who Have Multiple Disabilities ©2000 by Paul H. Brookes Publishing Co.

Recording Sheet 4-C

Child's name _____ Observer's name _____

Generalizing Turn-Taking Games

Describe the plan for each game, then record the results each time you play the game with your child.

Plan		Results	
Turn-taking game	New person or place	Date tried	How did your child respond?

PLAI: A Guide to Early Communication with Young Children Who Have Multiple Disabilities ©2000 by Paul H. Brookes Publishing Co.

Module 4 Summary

Child's name _____   Date _____

This recording sheet can help you summarize what you've learned about your child by completing the objectives of Module 4. Please share this information with your child's teachers and other caregivers.

Turn-Taking Routines that My Child Enjoys	
1	
2	
3	
4	
5	
6	

PLAI: A Guide to Early Communication with Young Children Who Have Multiple Disabilities ©2000 by Paul H. Brookes Publishing Co.

Module 5

Handouts

Module 5 Overview

Recording Sheet 5-A: Rejecting a Disliked Object or Activity

Recording Sheet 5-B: Increasing Initiation

Recording Sheet 5-C: Initiating Attention

Module 5 Summary

	Overview of Module 5: Encouraging Communicative Initiations
Rationale	The most important goal of this curriculum is for your child to begin to use or to increase the use of communicative initiations. An important prerequisite to the development of communication is your child's discovery that he or she can have an effect on the environment through his or her own voluntary actions. As you learned in Modules 1, 2, and 4, the most powerful motivations for children with disabilities to communicate are opportunities to obtain a desired object or activity, to obtain a caregiver's attention, or to reject something they dislike.
Goal	The main goal of Module 5 is to increase your child's use of communicative behaviors to initiate interactions in order to get attention, to obtain a desired object or activity, or to reject something.
Activities	You will learn to use several specific strategies in order to increase your child's communications. You will learn to allow your child to reject something he or she doesn't want or is tired of. Another strategy you will learn is how to teach your child to initiate by delaying anticipated events in the daily routine. For example, you can get your child ready for his or her breakfast, but delay it a minute or two. Finally, you will learn some ways to encourage your child to communicate in order to get your attention by setting up an anticipated event but moving away from your child so he or she has to get your attention in order to start the desired activity.

PLAI: A Guide to Early Communication with Young Children Who Have Multiple Disabilities ©2000 by Paul H. Brookes Publishing Co.

Recording Sheet 5-A

Child's name _____ Observer's name _____

Rejecting a Disliked Object or Activity

Disliked activity	How do you expect your child to communicate dislike?	How will you respond?	Date tried

PLAI: A Guide to Early Communication with Young Children Who Have Multiple Disabilities ©2000 by Paul H. Brookes Publishing Co.

Recording Sheet 5-B

Child's name _____ Observer's name _____

Increasing Initiation

First describe the plan, then record each time you try it.

Plan			Results	
Preferred activity	Usual sequence of cues	Where or how will you delay?	Date tried	How did your child respond?

PLAI: A Guide to Early Communication with Young Children Who Have Multiple Disabilities ©2000 by Paul H. Brookes Publishing Co.

Recording Sheet 5-C

Child's name _____ Observer's name _____

Initiating Attention

First describe the plan, then record each time you try it.

Plan		Results
What activity will you delay and how will you delay it?	What will you do while delaying the start?	Date tried	How did your child respond?

PLAI: A Guide to Early Communication with Young Children Who Have Multiple Disabilities ©2000 by Paul H. Brookes Publishing Co.

Module 5 Summary

Child's name _____ Date _____

This recording sheet can help you summarize what you've learned about your child by completing the objectives of Module 5. Please share this information with your child's teachers and other caregivers.

Ways in Which My Child Initiates Communication
1
2
3
4
5
6

PLAI: A Guide to Early Communication with Young Children Who Have Multiple Disabilities ©2000 by Paul H. Brookes Publishing Co.

Appendix E

Handouts in Spanish

ENTREVISTA PARA EL CUIDADOR DEL NIÑO/A

Nombre del niño/a _____ Fecha de nacimiento _____

Nombre del cuidador _____ Relación con el niño/a _____

Nombre del entrevistador _____ Fecha de la entrevista _____

El primer paso para mejorar las habilidades comunicativas de su niño/a es reconocer las maneras por las cuales su niño/a ya puede comunicarse y la frecuencia con la cual esto ocurre. Favor de anotar el comportamiento que usted ha observado en tanto detalle como sea posible. Esta entrevista tiene varias secciones. Favor de llenar todas las secciones.

Sección uno—Los sentimientos de su niño/a		
Sentimiento	¿Cómo lo sabe?	¿En cuáles situaciones?
Hambriento		
Incómodo		
Sorprendido o sobresaltado		
Feliz		
Triste		
Enojado		
Cansado		
Aterrorizado		
Sobre-estimulado		
Frustrado (se enoja durante alguna actividad)		
Quiere más de algo (p. ej., comida, una persona o una actividad)		
Quiere terminar una actividad		
Quiere estar con alguien		
Quiere estar solo		

PLAI: Un currículo de comunicación temprana para niños © 2000 por Paul H. Brookes Publishing Co.

Sección dos—Los comportamientos de su niño/a		
Comportamientos	¿Cuándo ocurre?	**Frecuencia** 1=Nunca/raro 2=a veces 3=frecuente
Hace expresiones faciales (sonríe, hace muecas)		1 2 3
Se ríe		1 2 3
Llora		1 2 3
Grita (y no lo puede calmar)		1 2 3
Berrinches (no le puede calmar)		1 2 3
Mira a la gente		1 2 3
Mira o toca objetos		1 2 3
Mueve su cuerpo (p ej., se inclina hacia adelante)		1 2 3
Mueve la cabeza para mirar a una persona o un objeto		1 2 3
Mueve la cabeza para oír mejor un sonido		1 2 3
Apunta o alcanza objetos o gente		1 2 3
Imita las acciones de otros		1 2 3
Hace gestos con los brazos o las manos		1 2 3
Hace signos para palabras sencillas		1 2 3
Hace sonidos (sin palabras)		1 2 3
Hace vocalizaciones (balbucea)		1 2 3
Otras cosas (describa)		1 2 3

PLAI: Un currículo de comunicación temprana para niños © 2000 por Paul H. Brookes Publishing Co.

Sección tres—Señales	
Tipo de señal	**Describa la señal**
Señales de tacto (p. ej., poner las manos de su niño/a en el agua antes de meterlo a la tina, tocar su boca para indicar "comer")	
Señales de objetos (p. ej., dejar que su niño/a tome la frazada antes de mecerlo con ésta)	
Señales auditivos (p. ej., hacer sonar un juguete cerca de su oído antes de dárselo)	
Señales de movimiento (p. ej., arrullarlo en sus brazos antes de mecerlo en la frazada)	
Señales de olfato (p. ej., darle a oler el champú antes de lavarle su cabello)	
Señales visuales (p. ej., mostrar la bañera al niño antes de bañarse)	

PLAI: Un currículo de comunicación temprana para niños © 2000 por Paul H. Brookes Publishing Co.

Sección cuatro—Las preferencias de su niño/a

1. ¿Indica si alguna vez su niño/a mostró una preferencia entre dos o más objetos? (p. ej., leche o jugo, mecedora o columpio). Piense de alguna situación o actividad que ocurra a diario como "jugar". Si usted le ofrece dos juguetes, ¿el niño/a escoge? Si hubiera más gente en el cuarto con usted, ¿su niño/a trataría de alcanzarlo o hacerle un sonido? Si la respuesta es SI, ¿cuándo?

   _____
   _____
   _____

2. ¿Hay algunas situaciones en las que su niño/a tiene que llamar la atención para obtener algún objeto o algo necesario? ¿Inicia su niño/a comunicación intencionalmente? Cuando usted está hablando con otra gente o está poniendo atención a otra cosa, ¿su niño/a trata de llamar su atención? Si la respuesta es SI, ¿cuándo?

   _____
   _____
   _____

3. ¿Hay alguna manera en especial en que su niño/a le responde a usted distinto a como lo hace con otras personas?

   _____
   _____

4. ¿Cómo calma a su niño/a cuando está molesto/a? Explique por favor.

   _____
   _____
   _____

5. ¿Hay algunos juegos (p. ej., "Encuéntrame", "Tortillitas") que le gusten a su niño/a? Explique por favor.

   _____
   _____
   _____

6. ¿Cuándo está su niño/a más comunicativo (p. ej., algunos vocalizan, alcanzan cosas o sonríen más durante actividades físicas y otros son más activos cuando alguien les da de comer)?

   _____
   _____
   _____

PLAI: Un currículo de comunicación temprana para niños © 2000 por Paul H. Brookes Publishing Co.

Análisis de un caso: La historia de Miguel

Miguel tiene 14 meses de edad. La historia de la mamá de Miguel, Cecilia, y de su hermana mayor Kate, será analizada a través de su colaboración en PLAI. Miguel nació prematuramente a las 26 semanas de gestación, pesando únicamente 1 libra 8 onzas al nacer y estuvo con respirador por casi dos meses. Tuvo varias complicaciones y procedimientos médicos durante su estancia en la unidad neonatal de cuidados intensivos, incluyendo una hemorragia intraventricular. Cuando él salió del hospital, se le diagnosticó con múltiples discapacidades incluyendo ceguero por causa de Retinopatía Severa de Prematuridad (ROP), aumento del tono muscular indicando Parálisis Cerebral Espástica y un grado de sordera no determinado.

Durante el primer año de vida de Miguel, su desarrollo fue muy lento. Se enojaba mucho y era muy difícil darle de comer, aunque ésa era el área en el que se había progresado un poco más. Por el momento, usa un chupón especial y toma hasta seis onzas de una fórmula adecuada para él.

MODULO 1 : Entendiendo las Señales del Niño/a

La rutina diaria de Cecilia era muy impredecible. A veces, ayudaba a su tío en una panadería cuando la necesitaban. Normalmente esto ocurría en la tarde o en la noche cuando Kate se podía quedar con Miguel. Cecilia a veces cuidaba a los hijos de su hermana, la cual tenía problemas para encontrar quién se los atendiera.

Los eventos más predecibles ocurrían en la mañana temprano o en la noche. Basándose en el horario escolar de Kate, la familia se levantaba todos los días a las 6 de la mañana. Cecilia preparaba el desayuno para Kate, despertaba a Miguel y le daba su botella. Cuando Kate se iba a la escuela, Cecilia bañaba a Miguel y lo vestía. Durante el resto del día, nunca se hacía lo mismo hasta que llegaba la noche. Kate o Cecilia le daban su botella a Miguel. A veces, Kate lo arrullaba para dormirlo mientras veía la televisión.

Cuando se les preguntó acerca del último objetivo del Módulo 1, ellas estaban muy seguras de cómo Miguel expresaba interés y placer: él extendía sus brazos y piernas, colocaba su cabeza hacia el centro y hacia abajo y no se movía. Ellas aprendieron a reconocer que antes de que él empezara a llorar primero se enojaba: ponía su cabeza en medio, extendía sus piernas y cerraba sus manos.

Cuando Cecilia empezó a observar las reacciones de Miguel en las actividades familiares diarias, se dió cuenta que cuando iba a levantarlo de su cuna, aún antes de que dijera algo, él extendía sus piernas y sus brazos. Ella no sabía como el niño podía sentir su presencia. Quizás él podía olerla. Al principio, ella pensó que se lo estaba imaginando, pero cuando empezó a llenar la Hoja de Registro 1-C: Observación de las Respuestas de Su Niño/a en las Actividades Diarias y después de haber observado varias veces, se dió cuenta de que la reacción siempre era la misma. El siempre hacía lo mismo cuando ella se acercaba a la cuna. También descubrió otra cosa. En la noche, cuando Kate le daba su botella, le costaba trabajo adaptarse a un ritmo estable al succionar el chupón y escupía más. Cuando Cecilia le daba la botella, esto casi nunca sucedía. Cecilia le dijo a la intervencionista que no sabía que pensar al respecto. Ella quería que Kate quisiera mucho a Miguel y no quería mencionarle lo que había descubierto para que no se sintiera mal. Pero al mismo tiempo, le daba gusto saber que Miguel reconocía su presencia y que parecía darse cuenta de que ella era alguien especial para él.

Después de descubrir que Miguel respondía consistentemente extendiendo sus brazos y piernas cuando ella se acercaba a la cuna, Cecilia y Kate estaban felices de empezar a trabajar en el tercer objetivo del Módulo 1 para ver si descubrían otras cosas que no sabían aún acerca de Miguel. La intervencionista ayudó a Kate y a Cecilia a notar que cuando Miguel (sentado en su silla) estaba relajado y sin poner atención, su cabeza estaba hacia un lado y reclinada para abajo. Cuando él estaba alerta y poniendo atención, él extendía sus brazos y piernas un poco y movía su cabeza hacia el centro aunque la dejaba reclinada para abajo. Cecilia decía que aunque ella sabía que Miguel no podía ver, era difícil pensar que él podía poner atención si su cabeza estaba hacia abajo. En el transcurso de sus observaciones, ella descubrió que cuando él levantaba la cabeza, era porque se estaba enojando y con berrinche. Cuando se ponía más tenso, él levantaba su cabeza por un momento y empezaba a quejarse y a llorar inmediatamente.

Cecilia descubrió también otra respuesta. Cuando le agarraba las manos a Miguel y le masajeaba los dedos (lo cual ella siempre pensó que a él le gustaba), él levantaba la cabeza y apretaba las manos. Pero cuando ella le masajeaba los hombros y su espalda, sus manos se relajaban y su cabeza se ponía en medio y hacia abajo. Ella se dió cuenta que a él le gustaba que lo tocaran en esa parte de su cuerpo y que en cambio sus manos eran extremadamente sensibles al tacto.

Cecilia sabía que Miguel no hacía cosas a propósito para llamar su atención y por lo tanto ella pensaba que Miguel ni siquiera sabía que ella existía. Cuando la intervencionista comentó con Cecilia el cuarto objetivo del Módulo 1 le dijo que este proceso podía tomar tiempo antes de que Miguel pudiera hacerlo- esto normalmente le toma más tiempo de aprender a un infante con discapacidades. Después de completar los objetivos en el Módulo I, Kate y Cecilia sentían que conocían mejor a Miguel.

MODULO 2: Identificación de las preferencias de su niño/a

Después de haber estado observando y aprendiendo más acerca de las señales de Miguel, Cecilia y Kate no tuvieron ningún problema en llenar la Hoja de Registro 2-A: Las Preferencias de Su Niño/a. Las cosas favoritas de Miguel eran: su mamá, pan de canela, masaje en los hombros y arrullarse en los brazos de Kate. No le gustaban las frutas cítricas, estar desnudo y meterse al agua. También le molestaba un poco que le tocaran las manos y los ruidos fuertes o repentinos. Al descubrir las reacciones de Miguel a los ruidos, la intervencionista sugirió que quizá sería buena idea hacer una cita para un examen del oído en el que tal vez pudieran diagnosticar más claramente cuánto podía oír y además hablar de la posibilidad de ponerle un aparato para el oído.

Kate estaba muy ilusionada por esta idea y usó su creatividad para presentarle a Miguel varios objetos y actividades para darse cuenta de cómo podía responder. Fue precisamente Kate quien descubrió que Miguel tenía un especial sentido del olfato y que habían ciertos aromas que le gustaban y otros que le desagradaban. Parecía ser que su aroma favorito era el de los panes de canela los cuales Cecilia a veces traía a casa de la panadería. A veces Kate podía calmarlo cuando le acercaba un pan de canela a la nariz y le daba a probar un poco de la canela y el azúcar. También descubrió que al bebé no le gustaban ciertas frutas como las naranjas y los limones. El olor o el sabor de éstas lo hacían que pusiera su cabeza hacia atrás y que empezara a llorar.

MODULO 3: Establecimiento de rutinas predecibles

En el Módulo 3, Cecilia tuvo la oportunidad de pensar acerca de la rutina diaria de la familia. La intervencionista le ayudó a planear los eventos diarios de una manera más predecible para ayudar a Miguel, así él se sentiría más tranquilo y en control de la situación y esto le ayudaría a entender lo que estaba pasando a su alrededor.

Aparte de la rutina diaria en las mañanas de levantar a Miguel y darle su botella, Cecilia decidió tratar de aumentar la predectibilidad de su rutina de la siguiente manera:

- Después de que Miguel terminara su botella, ella le daría siempre un baño.
- Después del baño, ella le pondría crema y le daría un masaje de hombros y espalda. Aún si era por poco tiempo, ella lo haría todos los días.

A la hora de ir a dormir, Cecilia le daría su botella y después Kate lo arrullaría para que se quedara dormido. De esta manera las actividades de la mañana y la noche serían más predecibles. Después de practicar en el próximo objetivo de identificar sub-rutinas, Cecilia se dió cuenta de que ella y Miguel ya tenían una sub-rutina la cual ocurría cuando le cambiaba el pañal. Después de quitarle el pañal y limpiarlo, Cecilia le soplaba en su estómago un par de veces diciéndole "ya estás seco, bien seco". Entonces ella le ponía talco (a Miguel le gustaba el olor), le ponía su pañal y le decía "ya acabamos" y le daba un beso mientras lo cargaba.

En el tercer objetivo Cecilia aprendió que podía ayudar a Miguel si añadía ciertas señales sensoriales a sus actividades diarias y a las sub-rutinas. Cecilia y Kate decidieron lo siguiente:

- Antes de entrar a su cuarto para sacarlo de la cuna, Cecilia siempre le diría "aquí viene Mami" en una voz fuerte. Le pondría sus manos sobre sus hombros antes de cargarlo.
- Antes de meterlo a bañar, ella pondría su pie en el agua un par de veces.
- Antes de masajearlo, ella pondría crema en sus manos y haría que Miguel lo oliera.
- A la hora de cambiarle el pañal, ella le daría a oler el talco y dejaría que tocara el pañal antes de ponérselo.

Aunque Cecilia al principio estaba muy contenta por estos procedimientos, se dió cuenta de que acordarse de hacerlo era más difícil de lo que pensaba. También se dió cuenta de que no veía ninguna reacción en Miguel y no le encontró razón para seguirlo haciendo. Aún así, ella notó que a la semana de que empezó con la señal de poner el pie en el agua antes de bañarlo, Miguel dejó de gritar cuando lo metían a la bañera. Pero ninguna de las otras señales parecían haber funcionado. Cecilia no lo hacía consistentemente y sólo se acordaba de hacerlo a veces. La intervencionista le dijo que no se preocupara pues podían pasar meses antes de que se notaran resultados en las reacciones de Miguel.

Cecilia continuó y hacía un gran esfuerzo en ser consistente. Después de cuatro meses ella notó algo interesante. A veces cuando dejaba que Miguel oliera la crema, él hacía unas muecas raras, que a veces parecía como si se estuviera riendo, lo cual podía ser posible, pues a Miguel le gustaba que lo masajeara. Miguel casi nunca se reía y cuando lo hacía nunca se sabía porque. Esta "mueca de sonrisa" antes del masaje le recordó a Cecilia como le gustaba ver sonreír a su hijo. Aún cuando la intervencionista le había explicado que este tipo de sonrisa se mostraba un poco más tarde en infantes como Miguel, a ella le encantaba observarlo.

MODULO 4: Estableciendo el tomar turnos

El Módulo 4 fue un poco distinto. En los primeros tres Módulos, Cecilia se había concentrado en observar a Miguel y en crear un ambiente más predecible y establecer el uso de señales de manera constante. Ahora, lo importante era ayudar a Miguel a aprender nuevos comportamientos. El primer objetivo ayudó a Cecilia y a Kate a enseñarle a Miguel a pedir más de algo que le gustara. Esto fue fácil de hacer usando el azúcar y canela del pan de canela. Kate lo dejaba que oliera el pan y después le daba a probar con su dedo. Ella le tocaba los labios y así él abría la boca. A través de este objetivo, ella aprendió que si le daba una probadita y esperaba, él abría la boca y movía su cabeza hacia el centro medio. Kate entonces le decía "oh, ¿quieres más?" y le daba otra probadita.

Cecilia también usaba esta estrategia cuando le daba su masaje. Después de masajearlo en su espalda y sus hombros por 30 segundos, ella paraba de hacerlo y esperaba. Como a los 15 segundos, Miguel levantaba la cabeza y extendía sus brazos para indicar que quería más.

Lo importante de éste módulo es ayudar al infante a aprender a participar en tomar turnos en las actividades y juegos, como por ejemplo en el juego de "Escondidas" (tapar los ojos y decir "¿dónde está Miguel?"). La intervencionista le explicó a Cecilia que era muy difícil para los bebés con problemas de visión y oído aprender este tipo de juegos. Cecilia se dió cuenta que a Miguel nunca lo había visto hacer eso. Así que decidieron practicarlo en una de las estrategias en el Módulo 4. Cecilia usó el "pedir más" al darle masaje y al ponerle crema. Lo que ella hizo fue reducir el tiempo del masaje a 2 o 3 segundos y esperar. A ella le preocupaba que él se fuera a enojar o frustrar. Pero para su sorpresa, parecía que él entendió que estaban jugando. Cecilia comentó que ahora él estaba disfrutando del juego tanto como disfrutaba del masaje. Lo mejor de todo es que en esta actividad Miguel siempre se sonreía.

Luego, Cecilia le mostró a Kate cómo jugar con Miguel. Miguel rápidamente entendió que él también podía jugar con Kate tanto como con su mamá. Cecilia también trató de que la intervencionista jugara con Miguel de la misma manera (al masajear y poner la crema). Pero a Miguel no le gustó mucho pues no era a la misma hora del día y era alguien extraño para él. Cecilia dice que Miguel tendrá que acostumbrarse primero a que la intervencionista le dé masaje y después poco a poco a jugar tomando turnos.

MODULO 5: Alentando iniciaciones comunicativas

Cecilia y Kate trataron de hacer que Miguel mostrara una señal de rechazo a naranjas y limones los cuales no le gustaban. Esto no resultó pues sus señales no eran muy consistentes.

En el segundo objetivo de aumentar iniciaciones tuvieron más éxito. Decidieron atrasar una de las actividades que a él más le gustaban: Kate arrullándolo antes de ir a dormir. Después de que Cecilia le daba su botella, Kate cargaba a Miguel y se sentaban en una silla mecedora y prendían la televisión. Pero ahora en lugar de empezar a arrullarlo inmediatamente, Kate sólo se sentaba sin moverse. Al principio, Miguel no respondió. Se quedaba quieto como tratando de ver que estaba pasando. Después, él extendía sus brazos y piernas y levantaba su cabeza como cuando se empieza a enojar. Tan pronto como él movía sus brazos, Kate le decía "¿quieres que te arrulle?" y se empez mover. En esta situación, Miguel empezó a aprender a pedir que algo empezara y no pedir nada más lo que ya estaba ocurriendo.

El último objetivo en este módulo fue muy difícil. Lo importante de este objetivo era enseñar a Miguel a llamar la atención aún cuando Cecilia no estuviera cerca. Como Miguel estaba vocalizando más, ella trató de hacer que él vocalizara cuando ella no estaba en el cuarto con él. Cuando Miguel estaba solo en su silla, Cecilia escuchaba como él vocalizaba. Tan pronto como él empezaba a vocalizar, ella iba al cuarto y le decía "aquí estoy Miguel. Ahorita te cargo". Desafortunadamente, la cantidad de vocalizaciones no parecían aumentar, y a veces cuando él pensaba que estaba solo empezaba a enojarse y a llorar.

Miguel todavía no ha aprendido a llamar la atención y tiene que practicar mucho. Aún así, Miguel y Cecilia han cambiado mucho desde que empezaron en el programa. Cecilia siente que ahora entiende a Miguel mejor. Ella conoce más lo que a él le gusta o disgusta y entiende mejor sus señales. Ha sido más consistente en como se relaciona con él y tiene más paciencia. A pesar de que a veces ella tiene muchos problemas, Cecilia espera a que Miguel responda. Miguel también ha cambiado mucho. Ahora es más claro en la manera en que se comunica. Su comunicación tiene un propósito en cuanto a Cecilia y a Kate y está vocalizando más. Pasa más tiempo despierto y alerta y hasta sonríe.

PLAI: Un currículo de comunicación temprana para niños © 2000 por Paul H. Brookes Publishing Co.

Module 1

Handouts

Resumen de Módulo 1

Hoja de registro 1-A: Horario diario típico

Hoja de registro 1-B: Categorías de estados de ánimo

Situaciones, antecedents, comportamientos y consecuencias

Hoja de registro 1-C: Observación de las respuestas de su niño a en las actividades diarias

Hoja de registro 1-D: Estrategias y propósitos de su niño/a en cuanto a obtener atención

Logros de módulo 1

	Resumen de Módulo 1: Entendiendo las señales de su niño/a
Razón Fundamental	Los niños se comunican de muchas maneras desde antes de que empiecen a hablar. Cuando usted responde e interpreta correctamente estas comunicaciones tempranas (p. ej., expresiones faciales, sonidos, señalar con el dedo, etc.) ayuda a que su niño/a entienda el lenguaje y lo anima a comunicarse aún más. Cuando un niño/a tiene discapacidades múltiples, (como la pérdida auditiva, deficiencia visual y dificultades con el movimiento físico) sus señales de comunicación son frecuentemente muy difíciles de reconocer y entender. Antes de que usted pueda ayudar a su niño/a a aprender nuevas maneras de comunicarse, usted debe primero descubrir todas las maneras en las que su niño/a ya se está comunicando, así como las clases de cosas sobre las que su niño/a está más motivado a comunicarse.
Meta	La meta del Módulo 1 es la de ayudar a llegar a ser un observador muy cuidadoso de las señales de su niño/a (señales que comunican los deseos y sentimietos de su niño/a). Al final del Módulo 1 usted tendrá un panorama bien detallado de como su niño/a expresa atención e interés, así como también de lo que llamamos "estado de ánimo" (p. ej., el estar alerta, soñoliento, contento, o enfadado) y de cómo responde a los cambios en el medio ambiente.
Actividades	Se han diseñado varias actividades para ayudarlo a practicar estas habilidades de observación y para identificar todas las maneras de las que su niño/a se comunica. Usted empezará por mirar más de cerca las actividades diarias de su niño/a. A través de una serie de cuidadosas observaciones enfocadas en un día común, usted puede mantener un registro de las respuestas de su niño/a hacia las personas y las actividades en su ambiente diario. Tambien se han diseñado varias formas para ayudarlo a registrar comportamientos comunicativos que pueden ser difíciles de reconocer y que podrían de otra manera ser pasados por alto.

PLAI: Un currículo de comunicación temprana para niños © 2000 por Paul H. Brookes Publishing Co.

Hoja de registro 1-A

Nombre del niño/a _____

Nombre del observandor _____ Fecha _____

Horario diario típico

Hora	Actividad	Gustos	Desagrados	¿Cómo lo sabe usted?
6–7 A.M.				
7–8 A.M.				
8–9 A.M.				
9–10 A.M.				
10–11 A.M.				
11–12 P.M.				
12–1 P.M.				
1–2 P.M.				
2–3 P.M.				
3–4 P.M.				
4–5 P.M.				
5–6 P.M.				
6–7 P.M.				
7–8 P.M.				
8–9 P.M.				
9–10 P.M.				
10–11 P.M.				

PLAI: Un currículo de comunicación temprana para niños © 2000 por Paul H. Brookes Publishing Co.

Hoja de registro 1-B

Nombre del niño/a _____

Nombre del observandor _____ Fecha _____

Categorías de estados de ánimo

Estado de ánimo	Descripción
Activo y alerta	Su niño/a trata de interactuar con otras personas (p. ej., mira la cara de su mamá, vocaliza) o con su ambiente (p.ej., alcanza un juguete, golpea la mesa) usando modalidades visuales, auditivas o táctiles.
Llorando o agitado	Su niño/a presenta vocalizaciones intensas, llantos o gritos. Su niño/a puede presentar gestos faciales o muecas con o sin vocalizaciones intensas y puede presentar aumento de tensión en el cuerpo o intensa actividad motora.
Distraído o no pone atención	Su niño/a está despierto/a pero no tiene orientación hacia el estímulo auditivo, visual o táctil. Sus ojos pueden parecer brillosos o tristes. Puede tener movimientos breves de su cuerpo o sus extremidades o sobresaltos.
Adormecido	Los ojos de su niño/a están abiertos pero los párpados parecen "pesados" o los ojos pueden abrir y cerrar repetidamente. Pueden ocurrir vocalizaciones.
Mantenerse en comportamiento repetitivo/estereotípico	Su niño/a se mantiene con movimientos que son estereotípicos, repetitivos o rítmicos (p. ej., mover la cabeza, sacudir los brazos, mascar o chupar, mecer o sacudir las manos).
Descontento	Las vocalizaciones de su niño/a o sus expresiones faciales parecen como de irritado, "queja" o incómodo, pero sin llanto.
Callado y alerta	Los ojos de su niño/a están abiertos y existe enfoque en el estímulo auditivo, visual táctil. Su niño/a puede mover extremidades o cuerpo un poco o sobresaltar brevemente.

¿Cuántos de estos estados ha observado usted en su niño/a?

Estado de ánimo	Cuándo

PLAI: Un currículo de comunicación temprana para niños © 2000 por Paul H. Brookes Publishing Co.

Situaciones, antecedentes, comportamientos y consecuencias

Esta tabla puede ayudarlo a reconocer los antecedentes, comportamientos y consecuencias con su niño/a. También puede ayudarlo a llenar la Hoja de Registro 1-C. Este ejemplo da antecedentes, comportamientos y consecuencias posibles a la hora del baño, la cual es una actividad cotidiana. Es importante notar cuando un comportamiento está relacionado con lo que pasa antes. A veces si usted cambia el antecedente, puede cambiar el comportamiento.

Situación
(¿qué está pasando?)
Hora del baño

Antecedente (qué pasa antes del comportamiento de su niño/a)	**Comportamiento** (cómo responde su niño/a)	**Consecuencia** (cómo usted responde al comportamiento de su niño/a)
La mamá de Joey lo desviste y lo pone en la bañera.	Joey arquea la espalda y llora.	La mamá de Joey lo cambia de posición.
La mamá coge el pie de Joey y lo pone en el agua, después pone a Joey en la bañera.	Joey hace muecas.	La mamá habla con Joey.
La mamá de Joey dice, "¡Es la hora del baño!" y lo pone en el baño.	Joey lloriquea un poquito.	La mamá de Joey lo calma.
La mamá empieza a lavar la cara y el pelo di Joey.	Joey grita.	La mamá le canta.
La mamá pone la botella de champú debajo de la nariz de Joey.	Joey se calma y se pone alerta.	La mamá habla con Joey.

PLAI: Un currículo de comunicación temprana para niños © 2000 por Paul H. Brookes Publishing Co.

Hoja de registro 1-C

Nombre del niño/a _____ Nombre del observandor _____ Fecha _____

Observación de las respuestas de su niño/a en las actividades diarias

Primero llene las secciones de situación y comportamiento y después pense en los antecedentes y consecuencias del comportamiento de su niño/a.

Situación (Actividad Diaria)	**Antecedente** (¿Qué es lo que pasa antes del comportamiento?)	**Comportamiento** (¿Qué es lo que su niño/a hace?)	**Consecuencia** (¿Qué pasa después del comportamiento de su niño/a?)

PLAI: Un currículo de comunicación temprana para niños © 2000 por Paul H. Brookes Publishing Co.

Hoja de registro 1-D

Nombre del niño/a _____ Nombre del observandor _____

Estrategias y propósitos de su niño/a en cuanto a obtener atención

Describa una situación en la que su niño/a estaba tratando de obtener su atención	¿Cómo obtuvo su atención su niño/a?	¿Que piensa usted que le estaba tratando de comunicar?	Fecha de la observación

PLAI: Un currículo de comunicación temprana para niños © 2000 por Paul H. Brookes Publishing Co.

Logros de módulo 1

Nombre del niño/a _____   Fecha _____

Esta hoja de registro puede ayudarlo a resumir lo que usted ha aprendido de su niño/a al completar los objetivos en el Módulo 1. Favor de comunicar esta información con los maestros de su niño/a y con la otra gente que la o lo cuida.

Entiendo las señales de su niño/a
1. Las actividades diarias de nuestra familia regularmente incluyen   _____ _____   _____ _____   _____ _____   2. La hora del día preferida para mi niño/a es _____   3. Mi niño/a se comunica de las siguientes maneras   _____   _____   _____   4. El propósito más frecuente de su comunicación es   _____ _____   _____ _____   _____ _____   5. Mi niño/a llama mi atención haciendo   _____ _____   _____ _____

PLAI: Un currículo de comunicación temprana para niños © 2000 por Paul H. Brookes Publishing Co.

Module 2

Handouts

Resumen de Módulo 2

Hoja de registro 2-A: Preferencias de su niño/a

Hoja de registro 2-B: Las respuestas de su niño/a a las personas, los objetos y las actividades

Logros de módulo 2

Resumen de Módulo 2: Identificando las preferencias de su niño/a	
Razón fundamental	La motivación es la llave para el aprendizaje. El saber qué le gusta o no a su niño/a con respecto a objetos, personas y actividades es muy útil. Los gustos y desagrados de su niño/a pueden ser usados para motivarlo a comunicarse al obte n er o rechazar objetos, personas o actividades. Ahora que usted ha completado las observaciones del Módulo 2, es más fácil identificar las cosas que más y menos le gustan a su niño/a. Más adelante, en el Módulo 4, usted aprenderá estrategias sencillas que le enseñarán a su niño/a nuevas formas de comunicarse.
Meta	La meta del Módulo 2 es la de desarrollar una lista de preferencias. Esta lista necesitará ponerse al día periódicamente a medida que pase el tiempo porque las preferencias cambiarán a medida que su niño/a madure.
Actividades	Las actividades del Módulo 2 son muy sencillas. Usted sólo hará una lista de la gente, los objetos y las actividades que le gustan a su niño/a, identificando los que él o ella especialmente quieren y los que le disgustan, identificando lo que realmente él detesta! Usted estudiará las respuestas de su niño/a a gente, objetos y actividades específicas cuando son presentados y cuando son quitados.

PLAI: Un currículo de comunicación temprana para niños © 2000 por Paul H. Brookes Publishing Co.

Hoja de registro 2-A

Nombre del niño/a _____ Nombre del observandor _____ Fecha _____

Preferencias de su niño/a

	Le encanta	Le gusta	No le gusta	Lo detesta
Gente				
Objetos				
Actividades				

PLAI: Un currículo de comunicación temprana para niños © 2000 por Paul H. Brookes Publishing Co.

Hoja de registro 2-B

Nombre del niño/a _____

Nombre del observandor _____ Fecha _____

Las respuestas de su niño/a a las personas, los objetos y las actividades

Antes de llenar ésta forma, refiérase a la Hoja de Registro 1-B para las descripciones de los estados. Note que no es necesario presentar y eliminar cada persona, objeto o evento. Repase la forma terminada para identificar: 1) diferencias en las respuestas de su niño/a en los diferentes estados; 2) diferencias en las reacciones de su niño/a a lo familiar y las experiencias nuevas; 3) diferencias en las respuestas de su niño/a a la eliminación y presentación; 4) qué es lo que le gusta a su niño/a y qué es lo que le desagrada y 5) cómo demuestra su niño/a estos gustos y desagrados.

N= una persona, un objeto o un evento nuevo   F= una persona, un objeto o un evento familiar

Estado de comportamiento	¿Qué le presentó?	¿Cómo respondió su niño/a a esto?	N	F

Estado de comportamiento	¿Qué le quitó?	¿Cómo respondió su niño/a a esto?	N	F

PLAI: Un currículo de comunicación temprana para niños © 2000 por Paul H. Brookes Publishing Co.

Logros de módulo 2

Nombre del niño/a _____ Fecha _____

Esta hoja de registro puede ayudarlo a resumir lo que usted ha aprendido de su niño/a al completar los objetivos en el Módulo 2. Favor de comunicar esta información a los maestros de su niño/a y con la otra gente que la o lo cuida.

Identificando preferencias
1. Las cosas favoritas de mi niño/a son   Personas _____ _____   _____ _____   _____ _____   Objetos _____ _____   _____ _____   _____ _____   Actividades _____ _____   _____ _____   _____ _____   2. A mi niño/a verdaderamente le disgustan   Personas _____ _____   _____ _____   Objetos _____ _____   _____ _____   Actividades _____ _____   _____ _____

PLAI: Un currículo de comunicación temprana para niños © 2000 por Paul H. Brookes Publishing Co.

Module 3

Handouts

Resumen de Módulo 3

Hoja de registro 3-A: Actividades diarias predecibles

Hoja de registro 3-B: Rutinas secundarias y senales

Señales tactiles

Señales auditivas

Señales de movimiento

Señales del olfato

Señales visuals

Hoja de registro 3-C: Los resultados de las señales nuevas

Logros de módulo 3

Resumen de Módulo 3: Estableciendo las rutinas predecibles

Razón Fundamental	Una de las cosas que ayuda a los niños a entender el mundo alrededor de ellos es la de tener un horario predecible. Al identificar frecuentemente las actividades que ocurren y establecer un orden consistente en el cual ellas ocurrirán cada día, se crea un sentido de confianza y control en su ambiente. El niño empieza a entender lo que va a pasar al reconocer ciertas indicaciones y señales que ocurren precisamente antes de la actividad o el evento familiar (p. ej., desvestirse y jugar a las "Tortillitas" antes de tomar el baño). Las sub-rutinas también son importantes. Estas consisten de sucesiones o pasos que ocurren dentro de una actividad familiar como a la hora del baño o al vestirse. Una vez que estas rutinas están establecidas, el uso consistente de ciertas palabras, sensaciones de visión y de tacto con cada actividad (p. ej., siempre le ayuda a su niño/a a sentir el agua correr antes de ponerlo en la tina del baño) con el tiempo su niño/a le dará significado a esas palabras o a otras indicaciones. Al hacer que el niño use al máximo sus sentidos (p. ej., el oler, moverse, tocar y probar) aumentará su habilidad para anticipar actividades familiares y eventos diarios. El uso consistente de estas señales ayudará también a aumentar su atención y con el tiempo le hará más fácil a usted y a su niño/a establecer una atención compartida hacia el mismo objeto o actividad.
Meta	Hay tres metas en el Módulo 3. La primera es establecer ciertos eventos predecibles dentro de su horario diario (p. ej., mecer a su niño/a siempre después del almuerzo y antes de la hora de la siesta). La segunda es identificar o establecer ciertas sub-rutinas dentro de las actividades que ocurren más frecuentemente (p. ej., seguir los mismos pasos y usar la mismas palabras siempre que cambie sus pañales). La tercera meta es para hacer el máximo uso de los sentidos del niño para ayudarle a anticipar y a entender estos eventos predecibles (p. ej., siempre tocar el revés de su mano con una toallita antes de lavar su cara).
Actividades	Al usar la Hoja de Registro 1-A: Horario Diario Típico, usted podrá identificar los eventos más predecibles en su rutina diaria. Puede aumentar la predictibilidad de su horario diario y describir también los pasos específicos de cualquier sub-rutina que ya existe que usted pueda usar. O puede crear una o dos sub-rutinas nuevas que le podrían ser divertidas a usted y a su niño/a. Otra actividad en la que usted pueé trabajar en este Módulo es la de identificar maneras de maximizar el uso de los sentidos de su niño/a para ayudarle a anticipar y entender una actividad.

PLAI: Un currículo de comunicación temprana para niños © 2000 por Paul H. Brookes Publishing Co.

Hoja de registro 3-A

Nombre del niño/a _____ Nombre del observandor _____

Actividades diarias predecibles

Primero llene la actividad diaria, después anote el tiempo aproximado, luego anote lo que pasa antes y después de que la actividad ocurre.

¿Qué es lo que usualmente pasa antes?	Actividad diaria	¿Cuándo?	¿Qué es lo que usualmente pasa después?

PLAI: Un currículo de comunicación temprana para niños © 2000 por Paul H. Brookes Publishing Co.

Hoja de registro 3-B

Nombre del niño/a _____   Nombre del observandor _____

Rutinas secundarias y señales

Use una hoja diferente para cada actividad en la cual agregará señales nuevas.

Actividad

Rutina secundaria	Señales que acostumbra hacer	Señales nuevas a agregar

PLAI: Un currículo de comunicación temprana para niños © 2000 por Paul H. Brookes Publishing Co.

Señales táctiles

Las señales del tacto son dirigidas al niño en una manera específica para darle a saber qué es lo que va a pasar. Estas señales son muy provechosas para comunicarse con los niños que tienen pérdida visual o auditiva. Las señales del tacto deben de ser precisas, percatables y agradables para que el niño pueda mantener la atención y anticipación de la actividad. Use una señal del tacto a la vez. Será muy difícil para un niño aprender el significado exacto de la señal si más de una es usada en una sola actividad o si la señal ocurre al mismo tiempo que él es movido físicamente para tener una acción recíproca. Ciertos tipos de tacto en algunas partes del cuerpo pueden provocar movimientos de reflejo en algunos niños y esto debe ser evitado. A otros niños les desagrada ser tocados en la planta del pie sobre todo si han tenido experiencias de intervenciones médicas. Por lo general, un firme o profundo apretón se tolera mejor que uno leve o muy suave. El tipo de tacto y lugar de cada señal debe de ser seleccionado cuidadosa y sistemáticamente.

Estas son algunas señales de tacto que pueden funcionar para su niño/a

- Antes de lavarle su cara a su niño/a, déle una palmadita en su mejilla.
- Antes de darle de beber de una taza, agarre su barbilla.
- Toque sus labios con sus dedos dos veces antes de darle el primer bocado de comida.

Estas es una señal manual que puede funcionar para su niño/a

- Antes de darle de comer, guíe físicamente a su niño/a a hacer la señal de COMER (señale co-activamente).

Estas son algunas señales de objetos que pueden funcionar para su niño/a

- Toque la mano de su niño/a con una toallita antes de ponerle en la tina de bañar.
- Al ponerle la ropa a su niño/a, toque su pecho con la camisa antes de ponérsela.

PLAI: Un currículo de comunicación temprana para niños © 2000 por Paul H. Brookes Publishing Co.

Señales auditivas

Aun en casos de niños con pérdida auditiva, en algunos casos tienen algo de residuo para oír. Es importante hacer uso de la variedad de señales auditivas. Los niños tienden a ser más sensibles a sonidos rítmicos o a entonaciones exageradas. Para que el niño haga uso de los sonidos de señales significativas, debe ser eliminado lo más que se pueda el ruido de fondo de la televisión, la radio, el medio ambiente, etc. De esta manera, él se puede concentrar en la señales auditivas. Algunas clases de sonidos pueden ser muy molestas para el niño. Por ejemplo, algunos niños son extremadamente susceptibles al aumento de volúmen y pueden reaccionar de modo exagerado. Repentinos estallidos de sonido pueden causar que el niño se sobresalte y que llore. Algunos ambientes provocan sonido de eco que puede ser molesto y eso hace más difícil que el niño atienda a los sonidos específicos y que los localice. Por ejemplo, una cocina con piso de loza y sin cortinas sería un ambiente con mucho más ruido resonante que una sala con alfombra, cortinas y muebles acojinados.

Estas son algunas señales de sonidos que pueden funcionar para su niño/a

- Haga sonar la cuchara en un lado del plato hondo antes de darle de comer.
- Golpee ligeramente la taza en la mesa antes de darle de beber.
- Cante unas líneas del tema del programa favorito de su niño/a antes de prender la televisión.
- Agite el biberón de leche cerca de la oreja de su niño/a antes de ponérselo en la boca.

Estas son algunas señales de palabras que pueden funcionar para su niño/a

- Diga el nombre de su niño/a cuando vaya a darle algo o cuando vaya a tener una acción recíproca con él o ella o cuando lo o la vaya a saludar.
- En lenguaje sencillo, dígale a su niño/a lo que usted va a hacer (p. ej., "Mamá te va a lavar la cara ahora").
- Use palabras claves sencillas como señales (p. ej., "lavar" o "cena").

PLAI: Un currículo de comunicación temprana para niños © 2000 por Paul H. Brookes Publishing Co.

Señales de movimiento

Las señales de movimiento son una combinación de movimiento y sensación táctil. Consisten en mover o colocar a su niño/a de cierta manera que esté asociada con la actividad. Si un niño tiene Parálisis Cerebral, estas señales deben ser elegidas de acuerdo a su tono muscular. Los niños con tono flácido (hipotonía) tienden a amoldarse fácilmente pero es difícil mantenerlos alerta. Ellos se benefician con la estimulación física y posiciones que aumenten su tono muscular y que los mantenga alerta. Los niños con demasiado tono muscular (hipertonía) se irritan y son difíciles de cargar. Ciertas posiciones y maneras de cargar ayudan a reducir el tono y a mejorar la calidad, cantidad y área de movimiento del niño. Las señales de movimiento no deben ser usadas si proporcionan movimientos reflexivos o involuntarios (p. ej., si al voltear su cabeza a un lado hace que el niño mueva sus piernas y brazos al mismo lado o si al acurrucarlo sin una posición correcta hace que extienda sus extremidades y su torso.) En general, mantener con soporte a su niño/a al moverlo ayuda a que mantenga una posición simétrica y flexionada.

Estas son algunas señales de movimiento total del cuerpo que pueden funcionar para su niño/a

- Antes de sentarse a arrullar a su niño/a, arrúllelo mientras lo carga sobre su hombro.
- Cárguelo y menéelo muy despacio antes de ponerlo en el columpio.

Estas son algunas señales de movimiento de una extremidad que pueden funcionar para su niño/a

- Antes de levantar a su niño/a de la silla de comer, levante sus codos muy suavemente.
- Levante sus brazos sobre su cabeza antes de quitarle su camiseta.
- Aplauda las manos de su niño/a una vez antes de jugar "Tortillitas".

PLAI: Un currículo de comunicación temprana para niños © 2000 por Paul H. Brookes Publishing Co.

Señales del olfato

Los aromas asociados con objetos y personas pueden ser usados como señales del olfato. Su niño/a puede anticipar que usted lo o la va a levantar si usted siempre usa el mismo perfume cuando lo o la carga. Algunos niños son muy susceptibles a ciertos aromas, mientras que otros ni los perciben. Observe cuidadosamente las preferencias y respuestas de su niño/a a los aromas. Algunos niños son extremadamente susceptibles a los perfumes y a otros aromas fuertes. Usted necesitará observar cuidadosamente para determinar si ciertos olores producen sobre-estimulación o una reacción negativa en su niño/a.

Estas son algunas señales de olfato que pueden funcionar para su niño/a

- Antes de lavarle el pelo, déjelo oler el champú.
- Antes de darle de comer, déjelo oler la comida.
- Acostumbre ponerse el mismo perfume en las muñecas. Antes de levantar a su niño/a, acérquese a la cuna y ponga su mano perfumada cerca de su nariz y luego salúdelo.

PLAI: Un currículo de comunicación temprana para niños © 2000 por Paul H. Brookes Publishing Co.

Señales visuales

El uso de color, contraste, luz y espacio puede hacer un objeto más visible para los niños con deficiencia visual. Los objetos pueden ser vistos más fácilmente cuando están sobre un fondo de color contrastante sólido y sin brillo. Por ejemplo, un tazón blanco sobre un mantel azul tiene mejor contraste que un tazón blanco sobre la charola blanca de la silla de comer de niños. La cara humana tiene bajo contraste visual y así un infante con pérdida visual puede tener dificultad para reconocer a su mamá de piel obscura y de pelo castaño, la cual trae puesta una blusa de color beige obscuro y que además está sentada en frente de una pared de paneles de madera. En este caso, el contraste se puede usar para hacer visible la cara de la mamá más facilmente, como ponerse lápiz labial o una blusa azul y sentarse en frente de una pared blanca.

Los estímulos visuales que distraen deben de ser reducidos de tal manera que la atención visual de su niño/a pueda mantenerse ocupada. Por ejemplo: algunos niños pueden ser distraídos de la actividad en la que se encuentren si miran hacia una ventana abierta con luz del sol brillante o tendrán dificultad en ver un objeto que es puesto entre otros juguetes o en una colcha estampada. Las señales visuales pueden ser presentadas dentro del campo visual del niño y éste debe de ser motivado a mirar al objeto y a tocarlo. El uso consistente y sistemático del color, la luz y el contraste pueden ayudar a su niño/a a organizar la información visual y a reconocer situaciones familiares.

Estas es una señal de luz que puede funcionar para su niño/a

- Antes de empezar una actividad familiar, use una linterna eléctrica en una área de poca luz para enfocar la atención del niño a un objeto específico que será usado en la actividad. Ilumine un juguete favorito, el biberón o su cara.

Estas son algunas señales de contraste que pueden funcionar para su niño/a

- Antes de poner a su niño/a en su silla de comer, ponga un plato hondo de color brillante en la charola de la silla indicando que es "hora de comer".
- Antes de poner a su niño/a en el piso, ponga un juguete favorito de color sobre una cobija de color diferente la del juguete para indicar "hora de jugar".

Estas es una señal de color que puede funcionar para su niño/a

- Seleccione objetos en blanco y negro y colores brillantes para usarlos en las actividades diarias de las señales visuales. Use una toallita para lavarse de color azul para indicar "la hora del baño" o seleccione un biberón amarillo o una taza roja para la leche de su niño/a.

Estas es una señal manual que puede funcionar para su niño/a

- Use un gesto convencional o una palabra clave para señalar una actividad. Haga estos movimientos con la mano lentamente y repita varias veces. Póngase una camisa de color sólido y con alto contraste para hacer que sus manos se vean más fácilmente.

PLAI: Un currículo de comunicación temprana para niños © 2000 por Paul H. Brookes Publishing Co.

Hoja de registro 3-C

Nombre del niño/a _____ Nombre del observandor _____

Los resultados de las señales nuevas

Anote las respuestas de su niño/a cada vez que trate de usar una señal nueva.

Fecha	Señal usada	Resultados

PLAI: Un currículo de comunicación temprana para niños © 2000 por Paul H. Brookes Publishing Co.

Logros de módulo 3

Nombre del niño/a _____ Fecha _____

Esta hoja de registro puede ayudarlo a resumir lo que usted ha aprendido de su niño/a al completar los objetivos en el Módulo 3. Favor de comunicar esta información a los maestros de su niño/a y la otra gente que la o lo cuida.

Estableciendo las rutinas predecibles

Estas son las actividades predecibles en el horario diario de mi niño/a.

Hora	Actividad

Estas son las actividades que incluyen rutinas secundarias consistentes.

Actividad	Rutina secundaria

PLAI: Un currículo de comunicación temprana para niños © 2000 por Paul H. Brookes Publishing Co.

Module 4

Handouts

Resumen de Módulo 4

Hoja de registro 4-A: Solicitar más: Planes de interrupción

Hoja de registro 4-B: Motivando juegos con nuevas formas de tomar turno

Hoja de registro 4-C: Generalización del juego de tomar turnos

Logros de módulo 4

\multicolumn{2}{c}{**Resumen de Módulo 4: Estableciendo el tomar turno**}
Razón fundamental	Para los niños sin discapacidades una de las rutinas de comunicación más temprana es la que llamamos "tomar turno". No mucho después del nacimiento, el niño y sus padres interactúan tomando turnos. Por ejemplo, la mamá sopla el estómago del niño, en seguida él se pone muy efusivo y patea y luego para. La mamá sopla otra vez y el niño toma su turno, luego para y espera otra vez. Con el tiempo, este tipo de toma de turno se desarrolla en juego como "Encuéntrame" y "Tortillitas". Sin embargo, para el niño con discapacidades el tomar turno puede ser más lento para desarrollar. El Módulo 4 le enseñará algunas maneras para motivar rutinas de tomar turno y juegos con su niño/a.
Meta	La meta del Módulo 4 es la de desarrollar y extender las rutinas de tomar turno con su niño/a.
Actividades	El primer procedimiento en este módulo será el de motivar al niño a pedir "más" sobre algo a través de la interrupción de una actividad placentera. Usted identificará las rutinas de toma de turnos existentes que ya hace con su niño/a y tratará de hacer que duren más extendiendo la cantidad de turnos. También aprenderá a crear rutinas nuevas de toma de turnos de dos maneras. La primera empieza con interrumpir una actividad placentera y luego se extiende el pedir "más" a través de varios turnos. La segunda manera es un procedimiento de imitación en el cual usted intenta entrar en la actividad que el niño ya está haciendo, a través de la imitación de sus acciones. Estos métodos animarán a su niño/a a participar en juegos de toma de turno nuevos.

PLAI: Un currículo de comunicación temprana para niños © 2000 por Paul H. Brookes Publishing Co.

Hoja de registro 4-A

Nombre del niño/a _____ Nombre del observandor _____

Solicitar más: Planes de interrupción

Describa el plan para interrumpir las actividades preferidas de su niño/a, después anote los resultados cada vez que use este plan.

Plan			Resultados	
Actividad preferida	¿Cómo interrumpirá esta actividad?	Fecha del intento	¿Cómo respondió su niño/a?	Comentarios

PLAI: Un currículo de comunicación temprana para niños © 2000 por Paul H. Brookes Publishing Co.

Hoja de registro 4-B

Nombre del niño/a _____ Nombre del observandor _____

Motivando juegos con nuevas formas de tomar turno

Describa el plan para cada juego, después anote los resultados cada vez que usted juega el juegue con su niño/a.

Plan		Resultados	
Actividad preferida	¿Qué es lo que usted hará?	Fecha del intento	Respuesta de su niño/a

PLAI: Un currículo de comunicación temprana para niños © 2000 por Paul H. Brookes Publishing Co.

Hoja de registro 4-C

Nombre del niño/a _____ Nombre del observador _____

Generalización del juego de tomar turnos

Anote el juego y la persona o el lugar nuevo, después anote los resultados cada vez.

Plan		Resultados
Juego de toma de turno	Persona o lugar nuevo	Fecha del intento	Cómo respondió su niño/a

PLAI: Un currículo de comunicación temprana para niños © 2000 por Paul H. Brookes Publishing Co.

Logros de módulo 4

Nombre del niño/a _____ Fecha _____

Esta hoja de registro puede ayudarlo a resumir lo que usted ha aprendido de su niño/a al completar los objetivos en el Módulo 4. Favor de comunicar esta información a los maestros de su niño/a y la otra gente que la o lo cuida.

	Rutinas de toma de turno que le gustan a mi niño/a le gusta
1	
2	
3	
4	
5	
6	

PLAI: Un currículo de comunicación temprana para niños © 2000 por Paul H. Brookes Publishing Co.

Module 5

Handouts

Resumen de Módulo 5

Hoja de registro 5-A: Rechazando un objeto o actividad que le desagrada

Hoja de registro 5-B: Aumentando la iniciación

Hoja de registro 5-C: Inciando atención

Logros de módulo 4

Resumen de Módulo 5: Estimulando las iniciaciones comunicativas	
Razón fundamental	La meta más importante de este currículo es la de que su niño/a empiece a usar o aumentar el uso de iniciaciones para comunicarse. Un pre-requisito importante hacia el desarrollo de comunicación es el descubrimiento de que el niño puede tener un efecto en el mundo alrededor de él a través de sus propias acciones voluntarias. Usted aprendió en los Módulos 1 y 2 que las motivaciones más poderosas por las que los niños se comunican son las oportunidades para obtener un objeto deseado o una actividad, para obtener la atención de las personas que los atienden o para rechazar alguna cosa que les disgusta.
Meta	La meta principal del Módulo 5 es el aumentar el uso de conductas comunicativas de su niño/a para iniciar interacciones que obtengan atención, un objeto deseado, una actividad o para rechazar alguna cosa.
Actividades	Usted aprenderá a usar varias estrategias específicas para aumentar la comunicación de su niño/a. También, aprenderá a animar a su niño/a a pedir "más" de alguna cosa al interrumpir una actividad placentera. Usted puede también permitirle a su niño/a rechazar alguna cosa que él o ella no quiere o de la cual está cansado/a. Otra estrategia que aprenderá es la de cómo enseñar a su niño/a a iniciar algo cuando usted retrasa los eventos esperados por su niño/a en la rutina diaria. Por ejemplo, usted puede tener a su niño/a listo para el desayuno pero poede atrasarlo un minuto o dos. Finalmente, usted aprenderá algunas maneras de motivar a su niño/a a comunicarse para obtener su atención, estableciendo un evento esperado, pero alejándose de su niño/a para que de esa manera él o ella obtenga su atención para poder empezar una actividad deseada.

PLAI: Un currículo de comunicación temprana para niños © 2000 por Paul H. Brookes Publishing Co.

Hoja de registro 5-A

Nombre del niño/a _____ Nombre del observandor _____

Rechazando un objeto o actividad que le desagrada

Actividad que le desagrada	¿Cómo espera que su niño/a le comunique lo que le desagrada?	¿Cómo responderá usted?	Fecha del intento

PLAI: Un currículo de comunicación temprana para niños © 2000 por Paul H. Brookes Publishing Co.

Hoja de registro 5-B

Nombre del niño/a _____ Nombre del observador _____

Aumentando la iniciación

Primero describa el plan, después anote cada vez que usted lo intenta.

Plan			Resultados	
Actividad preferida	Señales de sucesiones usuales	Dónde o cómo lo atrasará usted	Fecha del intento	¿Cómo respondió su niño/a?

PLAI: Un currículo de comunicación temprana para niños © 2000 por Paul H. Brookes Publishing Co.

Hoja de registro 5-C

Nombre del niño/a _____ Nombre del observandor _____

Iniciando atención

Primero describa el plan, después anote cada vez que lo intenta.

Plan		Resultados	
Actividad que usted atrasará y cómo la atrasará	¿Que hará mientras atrasa el inicio?	Fecha del intento	¿Cómo respondió su niño/a?

PLAI: Un currículo de comunicación temprana para niños © 2000 por Paul H. Brookes Publishing Co.

Logros de módulo 5

Nombre del niño/a _____ Fecha _____

Esta hoja de registro puede ayudarlo a resumir lo que usted ha aprendido de su niño/a al completar los objetivos en el Módulo 5. Favor de comunicar esta información a los maestros de su niño/a y la otra gente que la o lo cuida.

	Maneras en las cuales mi niño/a inicia comunicación
1	
2	
3	
4	
5	
6	

PLAI: Un currículo de comunicación temprana para niños © 2000 por Paul H. Brookes Publishing Co.